Melville
and His World

Melville
and His World
by
Gay Wilson Allen

A Studio Book

The Viking Press ● New York

To
Edwin Haviland Miller
friend and colleague

Sunday afternoon on the Battery during Melville's childhood in New York.

Copyright © 1971 by Gay Wilson Allen
All rights reserved
First published in 1971 by The Viking Press, Inc.
625 Madison Avenue, New York, N.Y. 10022
Published simultaneously in Canada by
The Macmillan Company of Canada Limited
SBN 670–46740–5
Library of Congress catalog card number: 77–117066
Typography by Westcott & Thomson
Printed and bound in U.S.A. by Halliday Lithograph Corp.

Preface

Herman Melville's world encompassed a very considerable part of the known world of the nineteenth century. But it was the South Seas of the 1840s that gave him his greatest emotional experiences and subject matter for the books, about whaling, Polynesia, and life in the United States Navy, on which his literary reputation mainly rests. He was also in the South Seas at a dramatic moment in history. He witnessed the seizure of the Marquesas and Tahiti by the French Navy and the intervention of three great powers, France, England, and the United States, in the freedom of Hawaii (then called the Sandwich Islands). His conscience was also aroused by what seemed to him to be the exploitation of the brown people by the white race, in which the American and British missionaries played a part.

As a whaler and later as a passenger on his brother's clipper ship, Melville also visited Buenos Aires, Lima, Valparaiso, Callao (at the time an American naval base for the Pacific Ocean), and San Francisco, and formed impressions of their states of civilization. Before this he had sailed on a packet ship to Liverpool, where the social inequality shocked him, and later as an author he visited London, Paris, Cairo, Jerusalem, and the intervening tourist sights. Of course, the real story of Melville's world is not a travelogue, for his most important journeying was inward—to the symbolic world of his mind and spirit. This cannot be presented in printed pictures and must be experienced in the words of Melville's imaginative prose poetry, or poetic prose. However,

the visual images can aid the reader's mind in seeing the author's word images.

Mr. Peter Kemeny, my editor, has taken special interest in this first book in the series on a classic American author. His former assistant, Mrs. Helen Goldstein, began the great task of collecting illustrations and secured the cooperation of libraries and museums that had Melville artifacts and related materials. Her successor, Miss Mary Jarrett, enthusiastically took up the task Mrs. Goldstein did not quite finish. Other persons who have generously assisted in this work are: Mr. W. H. Bond, Librarian of the Houghton Library, Cambridge, Massachusetts, and his assistant Miss Carolyn Jakeman; Mr. F. G. Benjamin and Mrs. Ropes Cabot, Curator, of the Bostonian Society, Boston, Massachusetts; Mrs. Frances D. Broderick, Lansingburgh, New York; Professor Hennig Cohen, University of Pennsylvania, Secretary of the Melville Society; and Professor Edwin H. Miller, the editor's colleague at New York University. Institutions and staff members which have provided both information and photographs: Houghton Library and Fogg Museum, Harvard University; The National Archives, Washington, D. C.; the Gansevoort-Lansing Collection, Picture Collection, and Stokes Collection of the New York Public Library; the Bostonian Society; the Berkshire Athenæum, Pittsfield, Massachusetts; Museum of the City of New York; Walker Art Gallery, Liverpool, England; the Kendall Whaling Museum, Lynn Massachusetts; the Old Dartmouth Historical Society and Whaling Museum, New Bedford, Massachusetts; and the Albany Institute of History and Art, Albany, New York. (See also Picture Credits at back of book.)

For biographical and bibliographical information I am indebted to many of the Melville scholars and editors, but especially to Charles Roberts Anderson for his pioneer work *Melville in the South Seas* and to Jay Leyda for his indispensable *Melville Log* for chronology.

Oradell, New Jersey   G. W. A.
December 18, 1970

6   Herman Melville (1819–1891).

Melville and His World

Herman Melville, the author of the masterpiece *Moby Dick* and other great sea stories, was born near the shore of the Atlantic Ocean on August 1, 1819, at Number 6 Pearl Street in New York City. Pearl Street, the center for textile imports from France and England, at the time, made a half circle around the southeast side of Manhattan. Beyond lower Pearl was State Street, and across State was Battery Park, surrounded by the ocean into which the broad Hudson River flowed.

In 1819 New York was a city of scarcely one hundred thirty thousand inhabitants clustered near the tip of the narrow island. It was primarily a shipping port, the largest and most active in the nation, having outstripped Boston and Philadelphia after the War of 1812. Steamships had been in operation only a few years, and they still carried auxiliary sails. Most of the hundreds of ships anchored around the Battery and for a considerable distance up both the Hudson and the East River were old-fashioned sailing vessels. Consequently, the populated part of the island was rimmed with an almost continuous line of masts. Thirty years later these masts were multiplied in number, but the scene Ishmael recalls in *Moby Dick* was different only in extent from the one Melville had known as a child:

> There now is your insular city of the Manhattoes, belted round by wharves as Indian isles by coral-reefs—commerce surrounds it with her surf. Right and left, the streets take you waterward. Its extreme downtown is the battery, where that noble mole is washed by waves, and cooled by breezes, which a few hours previous were out of sight of land.

On Sunday afternoon all strollers were drawn to the water: "And there they stand —miles of them—leagues. Inlanders all, they come from lanes and alleys, streets and avenues—north, east, south, and west. Yet here they all unite. Tell me, does

The East River from

the magnetic virtue of the needles of the compasses of all those ships attract them thither?" Melville wrote this with some of the scorn of the experienced seaman for the landlubber, but the scene so graphically recalled was one of the first to register on his infant memory.

New York side, ca. 1835.

Herman was the second son and third child of Allan and Maria Gansevoort Melvill (the *e* would not be added until after the father's death). His brother Gansevoort was four years older, his sister Helen two years older. A fourth child, Augusta, was two years younger. His father, a well-groomed, serious-minded,

Herman Melville's father and mother: ABOVE: Maria Gansevoort before marriage. RIGHT: Allan Melvill in 1810.

vigorous man of thirty-seven, with a round, fair, clean-shaven face, was an importer of French goods—silks, gloves, ladies' bonnets, and other luxury merchandise.

Herman's mother was an attractive woman of twenty-eight, with a fair complexion, masses of jet-black curls, blue eyes, and mouth a little too large and nose too prominent for real beauty. But she dressed in fashion and carried herself with confidence, as might be expected of the daughter of General Peter Gansevoort, who had won fame in the American Revolution by his defense of Fort Stanwix (also known as Fort Schuyler). General Gansevoort had prospered in Albany and at his death in 1812 was reputed to be one of the wealthiest men of that Dutch city. Though he had five sons, Maria was his only daughter and he had given her a private education suitable for her social position. The Gansevoorts attended and liberally supported the Dutch Reformed Church, and were conventionally pious without being dogmatically sectarian.

Some biographers have presented Herman Melville's mother as a vain and proud woman. Her simple, matter-of-fact letters do not show these traits, but rather those of a practical, domestic wife and mother devoted to her Dutch relatives and her own husband and children. Allan Melvill was proud of his Scotch ancestors, whose lineage could be traced back to Sir John Melvill, knighted by James VI of Scotland and made Baron of Granton in 1580. Allan's mother was a Scollay, who traced her ancestry to the Orkney Islands and the kings of Norway. His father, Major Thomas Melvill of Boston, was also a Revolutionary hero who had been

Paternal grandparents: RIGHT: Major Thomas Melvill, in Boston; LEFT: Mrs. Thomas Melvill (Priscilla); BELOW: Home of Major Thomas Melvill in Green Street, Boston. The Major, who had been fire-warden from 1779 to 1823, was honored on June 20, 1825, by a fire drill in front of his house. He is shown at the lower left in cocked hat directing a stream of water toward the church.

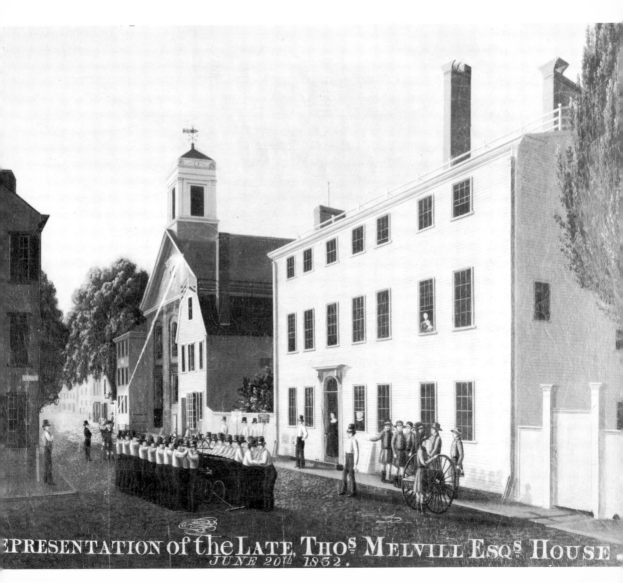

EPRESENTATION of the LATE THOs MELVILL ESQs HOUSE
JUNE 20th 1832.

ABOVE: Maternal grandparents: General Peter Gansevoort, in Albany; Catherine Gansevoort. OPPOSITE: Oil portrait of Allan Melvill by Ezra Ames, ca. 1820.

rewarded by President Washington with the office of Collector of Customs in the Port of Boston.

Three weeks after Herman's birth, his father wrote Major Melvill that New York had so far that summer escaped another outbreak of yellow fever, but that business was "absolutely stagnant." There were two reasons for his stagnant business: the whole nation was recovering from a severe economic slump, and since 1815 England had been dumping at bargain prices the textiles that had piled up in British warehouses during the War of 1812. As an importer of French textiles, Mr. Melvill was at great disadvantage.

New York City is nearly always hot, humid, and uncomfortable in August, but in 1819 the father of little Herman had serious cause for anxiety. In recent summers the city had been ravaged by epidemics of typhus and yellow fever, and several outbreaks of Asian cholera. The municipality had no system of sewage disposal and depended upon open wells for its water supply. It was still half-rural, with pigs running in the streets, and many barns for horses, cows, and poultry. Along with contaminated water and an abundance of flies, mosquitoes, and wharf rats, the city was extremely vulnerable to diseases brought in by ships from all parts of the world.

Soon after Herman was baptized in the South Reformed Dutch Church on August 19, "the alarum of fever" was sounded again, and his mother fled with

14

ABOVE: Steamboat *Albany*, Hudson River Line, in 1826. OPPOSITE: Oil portrait of Maria (Mrs. Allan) Melville by Ezra Ames, ca. 1820.

her children and a retinue of servants to Albany. His father remained in New York, but his store was closed by a quarantine extending from Old Slip to Wall Street. After cold weather arrived, the fever abated, and Mrs. Melvill returned. But the damage to Mr. Melvill's business was extensive, and he had to borrow money from his father, and from his brother-in-law Peter Gansevoort in Albany. Throughout Herman's childhood his mother frequently made the twenty-hour steamboat trip to Albany, and almost as frequently his father had to turn to his wealthy brother-in-law or less affluent father for financial help.

When Herman was a year old his father leased a comfortable house on Courtlandt Street, a block from the landing of the Hudson River Line. Once, when the boat arrived early in the morning, the captain of the Albany boat walked up the street to 55 Courtlandt to wake Mr. Melvill and tell him that his family had arrived. But in March 1824 the Melvill family moved farther uptown to 33 Bleecker Street.

During these years of Herman's infancy great events were reshaping his nation, and his own future. In the year of his birth a financial panic had altered his father's social world and increased the perils of his business ventures. The following year Captain Nathaniel Brown Palmer expanded geographical knowledge by discovering Antarctica. In March 1820 Congress adopted the Missouri Compromise, which prohibited slavery north of the thirty-sixth parallel, but only postponed the tragic conflict over slavery. In March the first American steamboat crossed the Atlantic, and the next year William Becknell of Missouri pioneered the Santa Fe Trail. In December 1820 James Monroe defeated John Quincy Adams for the presidency, and three years later proclaimed the Monroe Doctrine to protect American interests in South America.

New York Harbor from Bedloe's Island in early 1800s. In the summer of 1826, Herman sailed to a fortified island in the harbor with his father and Uncle John D'Wolf.

While these events were making history, young Herman Melville was growing up. In *Redburn* Melville recalled an outing in the summer of 1826 with his father and uncle (his father's brother-in-law) Captain John D'Wolf to a fortified island in the bay. The uncle had recently returned from Copenhagen, but he had sailed often to Archangel in Russia, and once with the explorer Captain Langsdorff had crossed Siberia by dogsled from Okhotsk to Saint Petersburg. Uncle John had white hair and a "handsome florid face." His home was at Bristol, Rhode Island, where Herman spent three weeks in the summer of 1828 with his aunt, Mary D'Wolf, while his uncle was on a voyage to Havana. Herman could visit the harbor and board some of the many ships docked there that the D'Wolf family owned.

Herman also went to Boston for long visits to his grandfather, who still wore his eighteenth-century tricornered hat, knee breeches, and silver-buckled shoes.

Several years later (1831), the young poet Oliver Wendell Holmes published a sentimental poem in which he called this old Revolutionary hero "The Last Leaf":

18

My grandmama has said—
Poor old lady, she is dead
   Long ago—
That he had a Roman nose,
And his cheek was like a rose
   In the snow.

But now his nose is thin,
And it rests upon his chin
   Like a staff,
And a crook is in his back,
And a melancholy crack
   In his laugh.

I know it is a sin
For me to sit and grin
   At him here;
But the old three-cornered hat,
And the breeches, and all that,
   Are so queer!

Major Melvill's house contained fascinating relics of the Revolutionary period, such as a bottle filled with the tea leaves that he had found in one of his boots after the famous "Boston tea party" (for Herman's grandfather had been one of those "Mohawks" who raided a British ship and threw bales of tea into the harbor as a protest against the tax on tea). But more fascinating still was a glass ship, kept on a Dutch claw-footed table. It was a model of an old-fashioned sailing ship, about eighteen inches long, of French manufacture, with every part made of glass —masts, yards, ropes, two tiers of black guns, and glass sailors in blue jackets performing their various duties. Herman would peep through the portholes to see what was inside, but all he could see was darkness.

In his own home, too, young Herman was constantly reminded of foreign lands by his father's bookcases filled with books in French, and portfolios of prints showing famous places in Europe. Herman and his sisters, Helen and Augusta, would pore over these prints for hours at a time on a quiet Sunday. At the dinner table his father spoke French to his Parisian butler, and not infrequently entertained French businessmen who conversed in their native language with their host when lingering on over expensive French wines and brandies. The boy who listened in wonder dreamed of the time when he would grow up, visit exotic places, and speak foreign languages. Three of Herman's Gansevoort cousins, Leonard, Guert, and Peter, were in the navy and wrote letters from romantic sounding places in South America and the Pacific Ocean.

Herman's Uncle Thomas, his father's older brother, had not only visited but lived in Paris, where he had made a fortune and married the adopted daughter of a great French banker and where his daughter, Marie, had been born. But Uncle Thomas had lost his fortune, later his French wife, and now lived with his American wife in Pittsfield, Massachusetts, on a farm which he was wholly unsuited to operate. Herman saw him pitching hay in his best Sunday clothes because he had no others. Occasionally he would stop, take out a satinwood snuffbox, and indulge in a stimulating pinch. Uncle Thomas was several times imprisoned for

ABOVE: Peter Gansevoort, Mrs. Allan Melville's brother, and Susan Gansevoort (Mrs. Peter Gansevoort). RIGHT: View of Albany, the New York state capital, familiar to Herman Melville in his childhood.

his substantial debts, to the chagrin of his father and brothers.

At the age of five Herman began attending school. His older brother Gansevoort was always at the head of his class and Allan Melvill thought him a genius. Of course, he did not expect Herman to do as well as Gans and was surprised when Herman, in his ninth year, won first prize in public speaking and distinguished himself in mathematics. The private school, the New York Male High School, was run on the English Lancastrian system, under which the master instructed a small group of his brightest students, and then each of these, called "monitors," instructed a group of eight in the lesson he had just recited. Herman further surprised his father by being chosen a monitor. The school year ended on August 1, Herman's birthday, and it was then that he went for a visit to his Grandfather Melvill, his Uncle D'Wolf, or uncles and aunts in Albany.

In 1828 the Melvilles lived on fashionable upper Broadway.

In 1828, Allan Melvill leased a charming two-story house at 675 Broadway, on "the fashionable side of the street," the fulfillment of one of Mrs. Melvill's ambitions—*to live on Broadway*. But the enjoyment was short-lived, for her husband's business difficulties increased and he was finally forced into bankruptcy in 1830. He was too deeply in debt for his father to rescue him, but Mrs. Melvill's mother and her brother Peter offered to help them. They moved to Albany in the autumn

In Albany the Melville family lived first on Market Street (now Broadway).

and lived in a rented house near the Gansevoort mansion. Herman's father was reduced to clerking in a fur store.

Uncle Peter was a trustee of the Albany Academy, and Gansevoort and Herman were promptly enrolled in this respected school. Its curriculum was no longer exclusively classical, and the faculty included Joseph Henry, who in 1829 had invented the electromagnet, which would in a few years make possible Samuel

Morse's development of the telegraph. Probably Herman was never enrolled in the classics department, because the records show that he did not study Latin his first year, and there is no indication that he began Latin his second year at the academy. But the second year he led his class in mathematics and bookkeeping, carrying off a prize for his achievement. Undiscouraged by his father's failures, he planned a career in commerce.

Organized athletics were unknown in secondary schools in 1830, but there

was bitter rivalry between the classical and nonclassical students, resulting in snowball fights in winter and quarrelsome encounters at other times. Later in Polynesia the savage raids upon each other of the Typee and Happar tribes could have reminded Melville of schoolboy feuds. For peaceful diversions there was coasting on the Albany hills in winter and swimming in the nearby Hudson River in summer. Not as fond of books as his brother Gansevoort, Herman found these outdoor sports more attractive than his studies.

BELOW: A grocery store in Albany, on an unfashionable street.
LEFT: Fashion center of Albany before mid-nineteenth century.

Clinton Park and North Pearl Street. During a brief period of prosperity in

Albany the Melvilles lived at Clinton Square and Pearl Street and kept a carriage.

ABOVE LEFT: Herman Melville enrolled in the Albany Academy in 1830.
ABOVE RIGHT: Herman's sisters attended the Albany Female Academy.

On December 30, 1830, the widow of General Peter Gansevoort died, and the funeral was held in the Gansevoort mansion, attended by the governor of the state and four hundred invited guests. In her will Catherine Gansevoort had deducted from her daughter's inheritance the considerable sums of money borrowed by Allan Melvill from her son. This still left Maria Melvill a respectable inheritance, but there were delays in settling the estate. Meanwhile, Allan Melvill was making an attempt to re-establish himself in business, but was in trouble again before the end of 1831. He then made a trip to New York and caught pneumonia. He returned to Albany, became delirious, and died on January 28, 1832. Later in the year Major Melvill died in Boston and it was found that he, too, had deducted in his will the $22,000 his son had borrowed—about the sum he would have inherited had it not been for the debt.

When Herman's mother finally received her inheritance from her mother's estate, it was sufficient (with some help from Uncle Peter) to set Gansevoort Melvill up in business as a dealer in furs, and for three years he prospered. Gansevoort now added the *e* to his surname and his whole family adopted the new spelling—*Melville*. In the spring of 1832 Herman, nearing thirteen, began working as a clerk in the New York State Bank, which his grandfather had helped found and of which Uncle Peter was a director. The family could now afford to live in a fine brownstone house at 3 Clinton Square, only two doors from Uncle Peter at Number One, where he had brought his recent bride, Mary Sanford, daughter of the chancellor of New York State. The Melvilles kept two horses and sent the girls to Albany Female Academy.

After working two years in the bank, Herman suddenly gave it up—perhaps because of eyestrain, his eyes had been weak since an attack of scarlet fever in childhood—and for nearly a year lived with his Uncle Thomas in Pittsfield, doing

28

the work of a farm hand. But early in 1835 he returned home to enroll in the Albany Classical School, clerking after school in his brother's fur and cap store. One of his teachers, Professor Charles E. West, later remembered Herman as one of his favorite pupils, who excelled in writing themes, and was "fond of doing it, while the great majority of pupils dreaded it as a task." He joined a debating society, read Cooper, Scott, Byron, and the seventeenth-century British poets—the latter being favorites of his sister Augusta. On Sunday the whole family attended church services in the old North Reformed Dutch Church across the street.

If the Melville family had continued living happily in Albany, Herman would probably have become a merchant and never thought of writing as a profession. But in 1837 Gansevoort was forced into bankruptcy by a national economic panic (started by a great fire in New York City in 1835) which destroyed major banks and insurance companies. His mother and Uncle Peter were nearly ruined in trying to save him.

Herman clerked in his Uncle Peter Gansevoort's State Bank of Albany.

The great fire in New York City
on December 16, 1835, started
a national economic depression.

Herman's brother Gansevoort.

BELOW LEFT: Lansingburgh Academy, attended by Melville in 1839. BELOW RIGHT: After Gansevoort's failure in business his mother moved to Lansingburgh on the Hudson. ABOVE: The Lansingburgh residence (house next to tree) of Melville family on River Street (now First Avenue).

32

Unable to maintain their home in Albany, the Melville family moved to Lansingburgh, a small town on the Hudson, ten miles north of Albany. To make matters worse, Gansevoort suffered a nervous collapse and was an invalid for nearly a year. Herman tried to help by teaching in a country school near Pittsfield, but the salary was only eleven dollars a month, the students were not interested in learning, and he found the experience very discouraging. At the end of the term he returned to Lansingburgh and took a course in surveying at the Lansingburgh Academy, a private high school, hoping to secure employment as an engineer on the Erie Canal; but this plan failed, too. In the spring of 1839 he contributed a series of sketches called "Fragments from a Writing Desk" to the Lansingburgh newspaper. He probably received little if any compensation for these juvenile essays and stories, but they furnish evidence that a newspaper feud with Charles Van Loon over the presidency of the local debating society had given him a desire to see more of his words in print.

Recently Melville's cousin, Leonard Gansevoort, whose parents lived at nearby Waterford, had returned from a four-year whaling cruise, and the tales of his experiences fired Herman with the desire to try his luck at sea. By May 1839, in the second year of the economic depression gripping the nation, Gansevoort Melville had recovered from his illness and was going to New York to study law with Alexander Bradford, an old friend of the Melville family. Gansevoort

promised to inquire about ships and send for Herman if he found a suitable one. Within a few days he wrote for Herman to come immediately. Accordingly, on a Saturday afternoon Herman caught an Albany steamboat for New York and stayed over Sunday with his brother at the Bradfords'. The next day Herman was to begin his first sea voyage.

Redburn is not an outright autobiography, but the novel was based on Melville's first experience at sea, and the sentiments he attributed to Redburn Welborne were undoubtedly his own, especially on his leaving home:

> It was with a heavy heart and full eyes, that my poor mother parted with me; perhaps she thought me an erring and a willful boy, and perhaps I was; but if I was, it had been a hard-hearted world, and hard times that had made me so. I had learned to think much and bitterly before my time; all my young mounting dreams of glory had left me . . . Yes, I will go to sea; cut my kind uncles and aunts, and sympathizing patrons, and leave no heavy hearts but those in my own home, and take none along but the one which aches in my bosom . . . there is no misanthrope like a boy disappointed; and such was I, with the warm soul of me flogged out by adversity. . . .

Monday morning, June 3, 1839, Herman Melville signed as "boy" on the packet ship *St. Lawrence*, under the command of Captain O.P. Brown. The

OPPOSITE: Lower Broadway. Gansevoort Melville returned to New York City in 1839. ABOVE: "Yes, I will go to sea. . . ." Herman Melville signed as "boy" on a packet ship to Liverpool. OVERLEAF: Melville's ship, the *St. Lawrence*, entered the Mersey on July 3, 1839.

St. Lawrence was scheduled to sail for Liverpool the next day, though high winds delayed sailing for another day. She was a small, three-masted, square-rigged ship, three-hundred fifty-six tons, with two decks, "coppered and copper-fastened." Unlike the *Highlander* in *Redburn*, she was only six years old, in good condition, and commanded by one of the better captains. It is unlikely that Melville, as did his hero, pretended to be the son of a wealthy gentleman sailing for his health, but he could not help feeling superior to the ignorant sailors and being shocked by their language and manners.

On Wednesday afternoon, June 5, probably at flood tide around two-thirty, the *St. Lawrence* cast off from Pier 14 in the East River, whipped by a cold rain blown by gusty winds from the northwest. Melville describes a similar scene in *Redburn*:

> The anchor being secured, a steam tug-boat with a strong name, the *Hercules*, took hold of us; and away we went past the long line of shipping, and wharves, and warehouses; and rounded the green south point of the island where the Battery is, and passed Governor's Island, and pointed right out for the Narrows. . . .

The boy's heart "was like lead," but he tried to cheer himself up by thinking that he was actually going to England, though not traveling as his father had. As the ship passed the fortified castle built by Governor Tompkins on the high cliff

ABOVE: New York Harbor as seen from the Bay in 1879. OPPOSITE: "Quitting the good city of Manhatto, I duly arrived in New Bedford" (*Moby Dick*, I). Fortunately 1839 was not as cold as the winter of 1835.

on the right side of the Narrows, Herman could not help remembering the time when he visited it with his father and Uncle John D'Wolf. Then "the sky overhead was as blue as my mother's eye, and I was so glad and happy . . . Then I was a schoolboy, and thought of going to college in time; and had vague thoughts of becoming a great orator like Patrick Henry. . . ."

After the ship had passed through the Narrows and the tugboat had turned around, leaving the *St. Lawrence* to sail on alone, "it seems like going out into the broad highway, where not a soul is to be seen. For far away and away, stretches the great Atlantic Ocean; and all you can see beyond it where the sky comes down to the water." It was hard to believe that "Europe or England or Liverpool" or any other place existed beyond that bleak, distant horizon. But Herman did not have much free time to brood on his loneliness.

At first even the names of the different ropes, sails, and parts of the ship were confusing, and the sailors laughed at his ignorance. But he soon began to perform his duties with increasing skill, and, slowly, won respect. One sailor named Jackson

39

ABOVE: The *St. Lawrence* arrived back in New York on October 1, 1839. OPPOSITE: Cenotaphs in the Seamen's Bethel at New Bedford gave Melville haunting premonitions of tragedy.

(Melville used the name in *Redburn*, but there was a man by this name on the *St. Lawrence*) affected him as a constant warning of what this kind of life could do to a man. Jackson was the most expert sailor on the ship, and the oldest, but the hard life and dissipation had left him nothing "but the foul lees and dregs of a man." He had recently had yellow fever and was still "yellow as gamboge." He was completely bald, his cheeks were hollow, his nose had been broken, he squinted out of one eye, and his rheumatism made it painful for him to sit on the hard chests. Herman felt that Jackson always looked at him with jealous malevolence because he was young and handsome—"at least my mother so thought me. . . ."

Fast packet ships made the run from New York to Liverpool in two weeks, but the slow *St. Lawrence* took twice that time. Finally, on July 3, "After running till about midnight," to borrow the words from *Redburn*, "we 'hove-to' near the mouth of the Mersey; and next morning, before day-break, took the first of the flood; and with a fair wind, stood into the river." In the misty twilight immense buoys went by, and shadowy shapes could be vaguely seen on the shore. "As we sailed ahead the river contracted. The day came, and soon, passing two lofty landmarks on the Lancashire shore, we rapidly drew near the town, and at last, came to anchor in the stream." The dingy warehouses lining the shore "bore a most unexpected resemblance to the warehouses along South-street in New York."

> At daylight, all hands were called, and the decks were washed down; then we had an hour to go ashore to breakfast [no cooking was permitted on the ships for fear of starting a fire in the crowded harbor]; after which we worked at the rigging, or picked oakum, or were set to some employment or other, never mind how trivial, till twelve o'clock, when we went

This Tablet was erected by
the Captain, Officers & Crew,
of the Ship Braganza
of New-Bedford.
In memory of
QUINCY A. HARLOW,
of Bridgewater Mass.
aged 19 y'rs, who fell overboard
Dec. 8, 1848. and was lost.

But why mourn his loss, or in sorrow repine,
For he's now at rest, in mansions divine;
Where the storm and the billow, shall assail him no more,
But with spirits made perfect, he'll praise ever more.

to dinner [at the sailor's boarding-house]. At half-past one we resumed work; and finally *knocked off* at four o'clock in the afternoon . . . And after four o'clock, we could go where we pleased, and were not required to be on board again till next morning at daylight.

Most of the sailors headed straight for the grog shops and brothels, both of which Liverpool had in great abundance, especially near the docks. Some old-time sailors said this was their favorite port, but Melville found the grime, the open sewers, the ragged beggars, the depravity, and people actually dying of starvation on the streets almost more than he could stomach. In industrial Liverpool the air was foul with coal smoke, the buildings were black with soot and grime, and everywhere contrasting evidences of opulence and the most abject poverty. Thousands of men and women, displaced by changing agricultural methods, had flocked to cities like Liverpool only to find no employment. The hordes of beggars appalled Melville, for at that time beggars were almost unknown in America (though a few years later, after the seaboard cities had been flooded by impoverished immigrants from Europe, parts of New York City would resemble Liverpool in 1839). For the first time, Melville began to see the need for social reform. He was made aware of the need not only by the conditions he witnessed but also by some of the street orators—especially Chartist reformers—whose earnestness made him pause and listen.

The hero of *Redburn* carries to Liverpool a guidebook his father had used a generation earlier, and is greatly disappointed to find that the city has changed so much that the old guidebook is almost useless. Melville *did not* carry Allan Melvill's guidebook, and he did locate some of the places he had heard his father talk about. Nevertheless, his first glimpse of a foreign country had none of the romance his imagination had conjured up.

On the return trip the *St. Lawrence* took longer than going over, because of prevailing head winds, but at sunrise on October 1 she was finally warped into her berth at the foot of Wall Street. After breakfasting at Sweeney's on Fulton Street, a place famous for Souchong tea and buckwheat cakes, Herman hastened over to the Bradford home on 19th Street near 9th Avenue, where he found letters from his mother waiting for him. Next day he caught a steamboat for Albany and arrived back in Lansingburgh either late that night or early next morning. Everyone greeted him with joy, but he soon learned that his mother's economic plight had not changed in his absence. In fact, mortgages she had signed were being foreclosed and her furniture had been advertised for sale. It was not a happy homecoming.

To Mrs. Melville's frantic appeals, her brother Peter replied that times were hard—though he did help to prevent outright starvation, and presumably some of her furniture was saved from the foreclosure sale. Herman began a frantic search for employment, and succeeded in securing a post at a school at Greenbush, a village thirteen miles north of Lansingburgh. For teaching a one-room school with sixty pupils he was promised a good salary, but it was not paid—or he received only enough to cover his board—and the school closed before the end of the term. After substituting in another school nearer Lansingburgh for a couple of weeks, Herman was convinced that schoolteaching was a hopeless way to earn a living.

Uncle Thomas had given up the attempt to farm at Pittsfield—though one of his sons remained—and had gone to Galena, Illinois, to try his luck in that frontier community in the northwest corner of the state near the Mississippi River. Lead had been discovered at Galena and the town was reputed to be booming. Uncle Thomas encouraged Herman to join him, perhaps thinking he might teach school there. Herman and a friend from Greenbush, Eli Fly, set out in the late spring or early summer of 1840 for Illinois.

Few details are known of Melville's western trip. Possibly the young men worked their way on boats, by way of the Erie Canal and the Great Lakes. Probably they found nothing to encourage them to remain in Galena, and after a few weeks traveled, perhaps again working their way, by steamboat down the Mississippi almost the whole length of the western border of Illinois to Cairo. In *The Confidence-Man* the steamboat pauses "At Cairo, [where] the old established firm of Fever & Ague is still settling up its unfinished business . . . In the dank twilight, fanned with mosquitoes, and sparkling with fire-flies the boat now lies before Cairo. She has landed certain passengers, and tarries for the coming of expected ones." In that interval, Melville's biographers speculate, he may have transferred to a boat headed up the Ohio River and by that circuitous route, most of it by water, returned in the autumn to New York City, still accompanied by Eli Fly.

At any rate, Melville was in New York in November 1840 looking for employment. Fly found work in a lawyer's office, doing copying, like Bartleby in Melville's later story by that name, but Herman either found no employment or nothing he felt like doing. Like Ishmael in *Moby Dick*, "having repeatedly smelt the sea as a merchant sailor," he took it into his head "to go on a whaling voyage." A few whalers sailed from Sag Harbor and Greenport on Long Island, but the center of the industry was in Massachusetts. Melville, his mind now made up, went straight to the center. Ishmael was determined to sail from Nantucket, the

43

cradle of American whaling, but the future author of *Moby Dick* was not so selective, though some of his experiences and Ishmael's coincided:

> . . . Some years ago . . . having little or no money in my purse, and nothing particular to interest me on shore, I thought I would sail about a little and see the watery part of the world. . . .
>
> I stuffed a shirt or two into my old carpet-bag, tucked it under my arm, and started for Cape Horn and the Pacific. Quitting the good city of old Manhatto, I duly arrived in New Bedford. It was on a Saturday night in December. . . .

Saturday night would have been December 26, so that Melville must have been

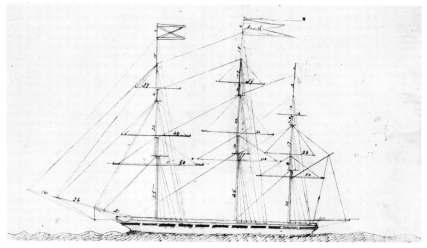

Architect's drawing for the *Acushnet*, in which Melville went whaling. (The *Acushnet* was a new ship, unlike the *Pequod* in *Moby Dick*.) OPPOSITE: Crew list of the *Acushnet*, with names of Herman Melville and Richard T. Greene, the "Toby" of *Typee*.

on the way, probably by boat, on Christmas Day. Records show that he signed his Seaman's Protection Papers in New Bedford the day after Christmas. He, therefore, spent the week end in New Bedford, much as Ishmael does in the novel, though there is no evidence that he roomed with a South Pacific ex-cannibal at Spouter-Inn, kept by Peter Coffin—though the latter is not unlikely. On Sunday, wrapped in his shaggy jacket called "bearskin," Melville struggled through a sleet storm to Seamen's Bethel to hear the Reverend Enoch Mudge preach to the sailors, just as Ishmael listened to Father Mapple in Whaleman's Chapel.

The ship on which Melville found employment was the *Acushnet*, a brand-new ship of three hundred fifty-eight tons, with three masts, two decks, a square

LIST OF PERSONS.

Composing the Crew of the _Ship Acushnet_ of _Fairhaven_ whereof is Master _Valentine Pease_ bound for _Pacific Ocean_

NAMES.	PLACES OF BIRTH.	PLACES OF RESIDENCE.	OF WHAT COUNTRY CITIZENS OR SUBJECTS.	AGE	HEIGHT. FEET. INCHES	COMPLEXION.	HAIR.
Frederic R. Raymond	Nantucket	Nantucket	U.S.	37	5 7½	dark	dark
John Hall	England	Nantucket	U.S.	30	5 11	Light	Brown
George W. Galvan	Fayall	Rochester	Portugese	25	5 9	Light	Brown
Daniel Smith	Philadelphia	New Bedford	U.S.	26	5 4	dark	Black
J. Warren Stedman	Boston	New Bedford	U.S.	25	5 2½	dark	Black
Thomas Johnson	Norwich N.Y.	New Bedford	U.S.	22	5 9½	Black	woolly
Enoch Read	Warren	New Bedford	U.S.	24	5 9	mulato	woolly
Joseph Luis	Fayall	Portugal	Portuguse	20	5 5	Light	Brown
Henry Harmer	Hebron N.Y.	New Bedford	U.S.	20	5 5	Light	Brown
William Barnard	Elizabeth City	Fairhaven	U.S.	25	5 5½	Light	Brown
George Vliet	New York	New Bedford	U.S.	23	5 6	dark	Brown
John Adams	Cape Verd	Fairhaven	Portugal	21	5 6	dark	dark
Richard T. Greene	Rochester N.Y.	New Bedford	U.S.	21	5 5½	dark	Black
John Wright			U.S.	18	5 5½	Light	Brown
Joseph Broadrick	Boston	Fairhaven	U.S.	18	5 6	dark	dark
Henry Brent	Portland	Fairhaven	U.S.	17	5 8½	Light	Brown
Virgin Wolcot	Stow M.S.	Fairhaven	U.S.	19	5 5½	Light	Brown
Carlo W. Green	New York	Fairhaven	U.S.	38	5 9½	Black	woolly
Wm Maiden	Philadelphia	New Bedford	U.S.	21	5 9½	dark	Brown
Herman Melville	New York	Fairhaven	U.S.	21	5 9½	dark	Brown
Daniel M. White	Scotland	Fairhaven	English	35	5 7	dark	Brown
Henry F. Harburg	Charlestown N.H.	Fairhaven	U.S.	20	5 9	Light	Brown
James Williams	Smithfield	New Bedford	U.S.	24	5 7	dark	dark
Robert Murry	New York	Alexandria	U.S.	25	5 4	Light	Brown
Martin Brown	Fayall	Fairhaven	U.S.	26	5 5	dark	dark
Alexander Barrow		_Additional List January 2. 1841_					
Alexander Barrow	Charleston	New Bedford	U.S.	34	5 11	dark	brown

Valentine Pease Jr.

I _Valentine Pease_ do solemnly, sincerely, and truly _swear_ that the above List contains the names of the Crew of the _Ship Acushnet_
together with the place of their birth and residence, as far as I can ascertain the same.

Sworn this _30th_ day of _December_ 1840.

Before me;

Valentine Pease Jr. Collector.

stern, no galleries but a carved scroll or billethead at the prow. The crew list for December 31, 1840, included: "Herman Melville: birthplace, New York; age, 21; height, 5 feet 9½ inches; complexion, dark; hair, brown." He was advanced eighty-four dollars on anticipated pay, so that he might equip himself for the trip.

Nearly everything in *Moby Dick* is symbolical, and the *Pequod* is more marvelous in appearance than the real *Acushnet*, but they were both similarly equipped for hunting whales and transporting the oil back to the United States. Captain Pease turned out to be irascible, but otherwise he bore little resemblance to the tragic one-legged Ahab in *Moby Dick*. The *Pequod*, for symbolical reasons, sailed from Nantucket on Christmas Day; the *Acushnet* sailed from Fairhaven, across the bay in New Bedford, on Sunday, January 3, 1841. But the season and the weather were alike—the freezing spray that "cased us in ice," the rolling hull, the screaming gulls overhead. The men "gave three heavy-hearted cheers, and blindly plunged like fate into the lone Atlantic."

But whereas the *Pequod* sails around the coast of Africa to the Indian Ocean (by Ahab's devious plan), the *Acushnet* leisurely cruised for whales in the South Atlantic, rounded Cape Horn, cruised for several weeks in the region of the Galápagos Islands on the equator, and then sailed over to the Marquesas Islands—where Melville deserted. The route and the places visited can be traced from the log of the *Acushnet* and the logs of other ships that held "gams" (a visitation between two ships meeting at sea) with her (Jay Leyda has collected this data in *The Melville Log*).

The polar weather in which the *Acushnet* left New Bedford lasted for a number of days, but gradually abated with each degree and minute of latitude of progress to the south. Though the destination was the Pacific whaling waters near the equator, west of the Galápagos Islands, a sharp lookout was kept all along the way. On March 13 the *Acushnet* reached Rio de Janeiro and sent back one hundred fifty barrels of oil by the brig *Tweed* out of Baltimore. Though not a large catch, this fact is evidence that Melville chased whales and participated in salvaging the oil during his first two and a half months aboard a whaler. Customarily, after a whale was sighted the men rowed out toward it in open boats, six men to a boat. They might chase the whale fifteen miles from the ship, and usually hundreds of miles from the nearest land. Within "darting" distance, the harpooner stood up and hurled his "iron" at the monster, whose head was nearly as large as the bow of the whale ship. Melville describes the scene in a review of J. Ross Browne's *Etchings of a Whaling Cruise:*

> . . . It flies from his hands . . . a mist, a crash,—a horrible blending of
> sounds and sights, as the agonized whale lashes the water around him

into suds and vapor—dashes the boat aside, and at last rushes, madly, thro' the water towing after him the half-filled craft which rocks from side to side while the disordered crew clutch at the gunwhale to avoid being tossed out. Meanwhile, all sorts of horrific edged tools—lances, harpoons, and spades—are slipping about; and the imminent line itself—smoking round the logger-head, and passing along the entire length of the boat—is almost death to handle, tho' it grazes your person.

But all this is nothing to what follows. As yet, you have but simply *fastened* to the whale; he must be fought and killed. . . .

If the men in the whaleboat survived this fight and conquered the leviathan—and many were mangled when with one slap of his mighty tail he smashed the boat to kindling—they then had to tow him back to the ship, often laboriously accomplished by three boats pulling together. Then, with the whale lashed to the side of the ship, there began the tedious and messy operation of cutting it up, boiling the oil out of the blubbery flesh, and sealing it up in casks.

Since the best whaling grounds were thought to be in the Pacific, the *Acushnet* made haste to round the Horn. Somewhere in the region of the Falkland Islands during a heavy gale Melville saw his first albatross, a "regal, feathery thing of unspotted whiteness," standing on one of the main hatches. A sailor said it was a "goney." At the time Melville had never read Coleridge's *The Rime of the Ancient Mariner*, but his own sensations were "mystical."

Rounding the Horn was always a fearful experience for sailors on a sailing vessel, and even in April, the beginning of autumn in the southern hemisphere, the weather was cold and windy. In *White-Jacket* Melville would recall the appearance of Staten Land:

> . . . Upon one occasion, the ship in which I then happened to be sailing [the "then" implied that it was not the *United States*, which provided most of the experiences for *White-Jacket*] drew near this place from the northward, with a fair, free wind, blowing steadily, through a bright translucent day, whose air was almost musical with the clear, glittering cold. On our starboard beam, like a pile of glaciers in Switzerland, lay this Staten Land, gleaming in snow-white barrenness and solitude . . . High, towering in their own turbaned snows, the far-inland pinnacles loomed up, like the border of some other world.

Throughout this trip, and even long before he had signed on the *Acushnet*, Melville frequently heard tall tales about a fabulous white whale variously known as "Mocha Dick," or "Moby Dick." In 1834 Emerson had heard of him as "Old Tom, who rushed upon the boats which attacked him and crushed the boats to

49

small chips in his jaws, the men generally escaping by jumping overboard and being picked up." In 1834 Jeremiah N. Reynolds returned after a five-year whaling trip to the Pacific and in May 1839 the *Knickerbocker Magazine* published *Mocha Dick*, based in part on his diaries, in which he had recorded the stories he had heard about this fabulous creature.

The monstrous albino whale with a scar on his head had already become a myth in whaling folklore before Melville began his voyage. But some of the stories of a whale chewing up rowboats, or ramming a whale ship, were based on fact. An English ship had such an experience in July 1840, and a Russian ship a month later. Doubtless Melville had heard some of these stories from his whaling cousin, Leonard Gansevoort, and others during "gams" on his own trip. In July 1841 the *Acushnet* gammed with the *Lima* from Nantucket, and Melville met the son of Owen Chase. The elder Chase had been first mate on the whaleship *Essex*, which a whale sank on November 20, 1820, when Melville was a year old. The following year Owen Chase had published a *Narrative* of the event. In a copy of this work, which Melville used while writing *Moby Dick*, he noted that: he had heard the story of the *Essex* in the forecastle of his ship; that the second mate of the *Acushnet*, an Englishman named Hall, had sailed with Chase (though not on the *Essex*); and furthermore, "about the latter part of A.D. 1841 [in July, according to the *Lima's* log], in this same ship the *Acushnet*, we spoke the W*m. Wirt* of Nantucket & Owen Chace [*sic*] was the Captain, & so it came to pass that I saw him." It is unlikely that Melville, a common sailor, talked with Captain Chase, but he did, his notes continue, talk with his son:

> But I should have before mentioned, that before seeing Chace's ship, we spoke another Nantucket craft & *gammed* with her. In the forecastle I made the acquaintance of a fine lad of sixteen or thereabouts, a son of Owen Chace. I questioned him concerning his father's adventures; and when I left his ship to return again the next morning (for the two vessels were to sail in company for a few days) he went to his chest & handed me a complete copy (same edition as this one) of the *Narrative*. This was the first printed account of it I had ever seen, & the only copy of Chace's *Narrative* (regular & authentic) except the present one. The reading of this wondrous story upon the landless sea, & close to the very latitude [the equator] of the shipwreck had a surprising effect upon me.

OPPOSITE: "Whaling in the South Seas"; the ship is towing a captured whale. BELOW: "Nothing was left of the boat but splinters. . . ." Melville heard many stories of wounded whales chewing up whaleboats.

A whaleboat struck by a whale's flukes.

Herman Melville could not have dreamed at the time just how deep that impression was, and that it would inspire him, a decade later, to write a masterpiece.

A few weeks before gamming with the *Lima*, the *Acushnet* had docked at

Santa Martha, on the coast of Peru. Sometime before leaving there on July 2 Melville wrote his brother Gansevoort, who received the letter a year later. To his friend Lemuel Shaw, Gansevoort wrote on July 22, 1842: "He [Herman] was then in perfect health, and not dissatisfied with his lot. The fact of his being one of a crew so much superior in morale and early advantages to the ordinary run of whaling crews affords him constant gratification." This assurance may have been written to allay his family's worries, but in any event in less than a year his "gratification" had vanished—as the ship neared the equator early in 1842—because of the heat, monotony, and bad food.

Happily, while Herman was abroad the fortunes of his brothers began to improve. His sisters started visiting Elizabeth Shaw—daughter of Lemuel Shaw, the Chief Justice of Massachusetts—Herman's future wife, though as yet he had no special interest in "Lizzy." If his thoughts dwelt on girls in the summer of 1841, they were not Boston girls.

After leaving Peru the *Acushnet* cruised near the equator for six months. In the fifth month Melville saw the Galápagos Islands for the first time. Those timeless, isolated volcanic islands six hundred miles from the coast of Peru, inhabited by strange birds and reptiles, had given Charles Darwin the first intuitions for his theory of evolution when he visited them while sailing on the *Beagle* six years before Melville's voyage. Of course, in 1841 Darwin was unknown to Melville; though three years later, while returning home on the frigate *United States*, he could have read in that ship's library the four-volume set of *Narrative of the Surveying Voyages of His Majesty's Ships Adventure and Beagle*.

Twelve years later, when Melville wrote his sketches of the Galápagos group, which he called *The Encantadas, or Enchanted Isles*, using the Spanish name, he had access not only to this work but also to several other explorers' accounts, and

Rock Rodondo in the Enchanted Isles, "two hundred and forty feet high, rising straight from the sea ten miles from land. . . ."—*The Encantadas*, Sketch Third.

it is difficult to separate the details he borrowed from printed sources from those he actually remembered from his visits. But he did set foot on those scorched and blackened rocks rising out of the ocean, which he described thus:

> Take five-and-twenty heaps of cinders dumped here and there in an outside city lot; imagine some of them magnified into mountains, and the vacant lot the sea; and you will have a fit idea of the general aspect of the Encantadas, or Enchanted Isles. A group rather of extinct volcanoes than of isles; looking much as the world at large might, after a penal conflagration.

Though most of the islands were barren, edible fish abounded in the surrounding waters, and whaling ships often paused to replenish their larders with fresh fish and monstrous sea turtles, which Melville called tortoises. The log of the *Acushnet* for October 30, 1841, recorded: "North head of Albemarle bear[ing] S.E. dist. 40 miles." This corroborates Melville's account of a boat's crew sent ashore on Albemarle to capture some tortoises. They brought back three, so large that they strained the ropes by which they were lifted up to the deck of the ship. They were "black as widower's weeds, heavy as chests of plate, with vast shells medallioned and orbed like shields, and dented and blistered like shields that have breasted a battle, shaggy, too, here and there, with dark green moss, and slimy with the spray of the sea. . . ."

A day or so later Melville was in one of the three boats that went fishing around Rock Rodondo, not an island but a round rock, "two hundred and fifty feet high, rising straight from the sea ten miles from land," like "the famous Campanile or detached Bell-Tower of St. Mark. . . ." From the water line to the top the rock was encircled by shelves in graduated series on which thousands of seafowl perched, creating a demoniac din, while others in great droves flew overhead in a continually shifting canopy.

> . . . The tower is the resort of aquatic birds for hundreds of leagues around. To the north, to the east, to the west, stretches nothing but eternal ocean; so that the man-of-war hawk coming from the coasts of North America, Polynesia, or Peru, makes his first land at Rodondo. And yet though Rodondo be terra-firma, no land-bird ever lighted on it. Fancy a red-robin or a canary there! What a falling into the hands of the Philistines, when the poor warbler should be surrounded by such locust-flights of strong bandit birds, with long bills cruel as daggers.

On these shelves also stood countless penguins, "like sculptured caryatides," "penitential" pelicans, gray gonies, gannets, and gulls of every variety. As day

On October 30, 1841, whalers from the *Acushnet* landed on Albemarle
in the Galápagos Islands to catch sea turtles for the ship's larder.

advanced, the din increased in volume. But underneath could be heard the
"clear, silver, bugle-like notes" of the "boatswain's mate," which Melville called
"the inspiriting chanticleer of the ocean."

The *Acushnet* circled in the vicinity of the Galápagos Islands for several months in the winter of 1841–1842, then moved farther west in the spring, but stayed near the equator, where whaling was thought to be best. The heat, the monotony, the complete absence of anything green except the mold in the dark interior of the ship, where everything smelled musty, began to sap the morale of the crew, and especially of Herman Melville, as he confessed a few years later in *Typee:*

> Six months at sea! Yes, reader, as I live, six months out of sight of land; cruising after the sperm-whale beneath the scorching sun of the Line, and tossed on the billows of the wide-rolling Pacific—the sky above, the sea around, and nothing else! Weeks and weeks ago our fresh provisions were all exhausted. There is not a sweet potato left; not a single yam. Those glorious bunches of bananas which once decorated our stern and quarter-deck have, alas, disappeared! and the delicious oranges which hung suspended from our tops and stays—they, too, are gone! Yes, they are all departed, and there is nothing left us but salt-horse and sea-biscuit.

Even the ship seemed weary, her scorched paint puffed and cracked, seaweeds trailing behind her, barnacles covering her stern piece, "and every time she rises on a sea, she shows her copper torn away, or hanging in jagged strips." But finally, riding easily in gentle but steady trade winds, the *Acushnet* dropped below the equator and turned southwest, to Melville's great joy:

> "Hurra, my lads! It's a settled thing; next week we shape our course to the Marquesas!" The Marquesas! What strange visions of outlandish things does the very name spirit up! Naked houris—cannibal banquets—groves of coco-nut—coral reefs—tatooed chiefs—and bamboo temples; sunny valleys planted with bread-fruit-trees—carved canoes dancing on the flashing blue waters—savage woodlands guarded by horrible idols—*heathenish rites and human sacrifices.*
>
> Such were the strangely jumbled anticipations that haunted me during our passage from the cruising ground. I felt an irresistible curiosity to see those islands which the olden voyagers had so glowingly described.

In this passage, again from *Typee,* Melville almost confesses that he had determined to jump ship and visit the "houris" before his ship reached the bay of Nuku Hiva. But whether it was the culmination of a secret plan or an impulsive giving way to his curiosity, the greatest experience of Herman Melville's life, and the most far-reaching, awaited him in the Marquesas:

Typee Bay in Marquesas: "There they were (the battleships of France), floating in that lovely bay. . . ." *Typee*, Chap. II.

In the bay of Nukuheva [*sic*] was the anchorage we desired to reach. We had perceived the loom of the mountains about sunset [June 23, 1842]; so that after running all night with a very light breeze, we found ourselves close in with the island the next morning: but as the bay we sought lay on its farther side, we were obliged to sail some distance along the shore, catching, as we proceeded, short glimpses of blooming valleys, deep glens, waterfalls, and waving groves, hidden here and there by projecting and rocky headlands, every moment opening to the view some new and startling scene of beauty.

. . . bold rock-bound coasts, with the surf beating high against the lofty cliffs, and broken here and there into deep inlets, which open to the view thickly-wooded valleys, separated by the spurs of mountains clothed with tufted grass, and sweeping down towards the sea from an elevated and furrowed interior. . .

In the spring of 1842 France was busy annexing islands in the South Pacific. But Melville, at sea for most of the past eighteen months, and six months away from the west coast of South America, was not aware of this fact:

Towards noon [June 23] we drew abreast the entrance to the harbor, and at last we slowly swept by the intervening promontory, and entered the bay of Nukuheva [more accurately, Anna Maria Bay; Nuku Hiva was the name of the island]. No description can do justice to its beauty; but that beauty was lost to me then, and I saw nothing but the tri-colored flag of France trailing over the stern of six vessels, whose black

60

hulls and bristling broadsides proclaimed their warlike character. There they were, floating in that lovely bay, the green eminences of the shore looking down so tranquilly upon them, as if rebuking the sternness of their aspect. . . . The whole group of islands had just been taken possession of by Rear-Admiral Du Petit-Thouars, in the name of the invincible French nation.

This experience, and subsequent events that summer of 1842, gave Melville a revulsion against the extension of colonialism by military power that would later provide one of the strongest themes in his literary works.

But on the day of his arrival in Anna Maria Bay he was distracted from his annoyance by the greeting his ship received from the natives. While still outside the harbor, a flotilla of brown men in outrigger canoes met them; others swam out with clusters of coconuts strung together and draped around their necks, so that the swimmer, his head in the center of the bunch, looked like a floating raft of coconuts.

Then came the beautiful sight of "whinhenies," to use Melville's spelling of the Hawaiian "vahine" girls, swimming out and climbing aboard by "seizing hold of the chainplates and springing into the chains; others, at the peril of being run over by the vessel in her course, catching at the bob-stays, and wreathing their slender forms about the ropes . . ." They all reached the deck in one way or another, "dripping with the brine and glowing from the bath, their jet-black tresses streaming over their shoulders, and half enveloping their otherwise naked forms." Somehow they had managed to bring with them a round shell filled with fragrant oil and rolls of white tapa. They assisted each other in drying off and anointing their bodies with the oil; then each girl draped a fold of tapa around her lithe waist. Now they were ready to captivate—"capture" was Melville's word—the crew.

That evening, the deck illuminated by lanterns, these "mermaids" danced their native dances with "an abandoned voluptousness" Melville dared "not attempt to describe." Although in *Typee* he would moralize on the corruption of these unsophisticated "savages" by "civilized" white men, he left no doubt how he and his fellow whalers responded to these winsome tempters:

> Our ship was now wholly given up to every species of riot and debauchery. Not the feeblest barrier was interposed between the unholy passions of the crew and their unlimited gratification. The grossest licentiousness and the most shameful inebrity prevailed, with occasional and but short-lived interruptions, through the whole period of her stay. . . .

But not even the enchanting "whinhenies" could take Melville's mind off a greater temptation. Thirteen years earlier his cousin Thomas W. Melvill, then a midshipman on the *U.S. Vincennes*, had visited the chiefs of Typee Valley with C.S. Stewart, who reported in *A Visit to the South Seas* that the Teiis (Typees) freely admitted to cannibalism. Herman must have heard his cousin discuss this subject, and he may have read Stewart (whose volumes he used later in writing *Typee*) before leaving home to become a whaler. In his novel he would use the threat of cannibalism to provide most of the suspense of his narrative. This conversation he reports with a shipmate may well have taken place:

I shall never forget the observation of one of our crew as we were passing slowly by the entrance of this bay [Typee] in our way to Nukuheva. As we stood gazing over the side at the verdant headlands, Ned, pointing with his hand in the direction of the treacherous valley exclaimed,

"There—there's Typee. Oh, the bloody cannibals, what a meal they'd make of us if we were to take it into our heads to land! but they say they don't like sailor's flesh, it's too salt. I say, maty, how should you like to be shoved ashore there, eh?" I little thought, as I shuddered at the question, that in the space of a few weeks I should actually be a captive in that self-same valley.

Melville did not, of course, desert ship to investigate cannibalism; rather he was so eager for adventure that he was willing to run the risk of meeting it. His excuse for desertion was the captain's tyranny, his neglect of the sick, and the starvation diet he inflicted on his crew. The fact that within two years, by official record, seven out of the crew of twenty-six men deserted lends some support to these accusations. But Melville was also the kind of man to seek adventure in the face of great peril. However, he did not jump ship impulsively, without preparations. First he wanted a companion, and found one in a small, nimble, courageous shipmate his own age named Richard Tobias Greene, called "Toby" by his shipmates. The night before—they were to get shore leave on July 9—they accumulated a quantity of sea biscuits, tobacco, and a roll of bright-colored cloth to barter with the natives. These provisions they slyly concealed in their sailor blouses next morning. Shortly after they stepped ashore from the longboat, a torrential rain drove them to a boathouse, where their companions soon dozed in the humid atmosphere. This gave Herman and Toby their chance to slip away.

They hoped to take refuge with the reputedly peaceful Happar tribe until their ship sailed, but they had no knowledge of the island and could only guess which

OPPOSITE: The "whinhenies" of the Marquesas were very amiable to sailors. RIGHT: Richard T. Greene ("Toby" in *Typee*) deserted ship with Melville at Nuku Hiva.

direction to take. As told in *Typee*, Herman was traveling with a badly swollen and painful leg, the result, he thought, of being bitten by a poisonous reptile. After a very steep climb over treacherous waterfalls, the two young men finally, after six days of hardships and hunger—water had dissolved the sea biscuits into dough flavored with the tobacco—reached a fruitful valley, only to find that they were among the Typees. This adventure, real or imaginary, Melville narrated in the first ten chapter of *Typee* with the tone of reality.

How much of the book is pure fiction? In 1867 the Reverend Titus Coan visited Nuku Hiva and checked on Melville's topography. He found that an ancient and well-marked trail led from the harbor over the mountains to the Typee Valley, about a four-hour walk, and that Toby and Tomo (the Typees' name for Herman Melville) were never more than four or five miles from the harbor. Even making allowances for their getting lost and Tomo's injured leg, it is not probable that they would have taken six days to cover the five miles.

In the novel Tomo lived with the Typees four months, learning to converse in their language, and making many ethnographical observations. Records of ships and consuls show that Melville could not have stayed with the savages for more than a month. However, unexpected support of the story came after the publication of *Typee*. Toby had left the valley before Tomo, hoping to effect his rescue, and by a series of fortuitous events returned to the United States. In ignorance of his friend's escape, he read the book, and through a newspaper in Buffalo, New York, corroborated the essential truth of the narrative. It is now believed that Melville did live with the Typee tribe for at least two or three weeks. He therefore based his novel on fact, though he magnified and dramatized his experiences for literary purposes.

Tomo's relationship with the nymph Fayaway (a very un-Polynesian name) is probably fiction, but the kindness of the so-called savages and their almost utopian society made a lifelong impression on the future writer. Why should he have wanted to escape from these happy people? In the story, there is always Tomo's fear that his hosts are merely fattening him up for a cannibal feast, but whether they did practice cannibalism he never did find out.

The world of the Typees was an almost unconscious world, in which the fruit of the tree of knowledge had not yet been eaten. The Typees were not acquisitive, either for knowledge or things, beyond their easily satisfied needs. Food grew on trees, or in the ocean not too far away, and they needed little clothing or shelter. They had time to enjoy eating, singing, being sociable, and making love. It was as near paradise as Herman Melville ever came, and he would never be the same again.

Native Marquesana in an outrigger canoe.

Whether Melville was actually rescued by the "five tabooed natives" (i.e., men immune to attack by other tribes) in the bloody manner narrated in *Typee* is not known, but the log of the Australian barque *Lucy Ann* confirms the fact that on August 9, 1842, the name of "Herman Melville, Able Seaman" was added to the crew list, and it is plausible that the Australian captain would have sent a whale-boat manned by "tabooed" natives to rescue a prospective recruit. How the Typees could have been persuaded to take their captive to the shore, if they really wanted to retain him, the author himself could not clearly explain in *Typee*.

Melville agreed only to "one cruise" in pursuit of whales. Official records also confirm Melville's statement in *Omoo* that the captain, H. Ventom, a pale, kindly young man, was ill and unfit for duty. In fact, so many of the details in *Omoo*, Melville's sequel to *Typee*, have been substantiated from reliable sources that this book can be safely used to trace the future author's adventures in the Pacific after he left Nuku Hiva.

The *Lucy Ann* (called the *Julia* in *Omoo*) picked up several deserters on other Marquesas Islands, and then set sail for the whaling grounds in the vicinity of Japan; but Captain Ventom became so ill that he had to order his first mate to sail for Tahiti. Before the *Lucy Ann* arrived at Papeete on September 20, Admiral

Du Petit-Thouars in the frigate *La Reine Blanche* had taken possession of Tahiti in the name of France after threatening to bombard Papeete if Queen Pomare, who happened to be in childbirth, did not surrender the island immediately.

Soon after dropping anchor, Captain Ventom sent for a physician on shore, and a Doctor Johnstone was brought back. He said that the captain must be taken ashore immediately for the safety of his life. The French had permitted the British consulate's staff to remain, and a "Mr. Wilson" was in charge as acting consul. The captain asked him to go on board the *Lucy Ann* and tell the crew that he had turned over the command to the first mate, James German, whose orders must now be obeyed. However, all the men hated German and many refused to obey his orders. Fifteen signed a "round robin" directed to the British consul, stating that they had not agreed to serve under German and would not do so. In spite of pleas and threats, the men, including Herman Melville, continued to resist German's authority, and they were arrested and sent on board *La Reine Blanche* to be placed in chains. They were told that they would be taken to Valparaiso for trial, but in a few days were removed from the French warship and turned over to the Tahitian marshal, a good-natured native known as "Captain Bob." He led the men to the "Calabooza Beretanee" (the English jail).

Calabooza Beretanee "was a mere shell, recently built, and still unfinished. It was open all round. . . . The only piece of furniture was the 'stocks,' a clumsy

BELOW: A scene on or near Tahiti, where Melville became a beachcomber. OPPOSITE: View on Tahiti, c. 1870.

machine for keeping people in one place." It consisted of two logs, the lower one with semicircular spaces hollowed out at intervals. The prisoners' legs were thrust through these semicircles and held there by placing the other log on top, kept in place by means of an iron hoop at each end. "This initiation was performed to the boisterous mirth of the natives, and diverted ourselves not a little," Melville declared.

One glorious Sunday morning Captain Bob waddled to the Calabooza and announced: "Ah—my boy—shippy you—haree—maky sail!" In plain English, the *Lucy Ann* had sailed, and from other sources the date can be fixed at October 15, three weeks after the mutiny—which was more like a "sit-down strike" than a mutiny. Even before the *Lucy Ann* sailed, Captain Bob's discipline had been extremely lenient, except for putting his prisoners to bed at night. Now he simply released them to roam at will. During the semiconfinement Melville had found a very amusing companion in the ship's doctor, who had also refused to serve under the first mate. No one knew his real name and the crew had called him "Long Ghost," as he was a tall, gaunt, but mischievous fellow with an "unscrupulous gray eye." Charles Anderson found evidence that Melville's eccentric doctor was real and not entirely imaginary, but he learned little more of his history than Melville gave in *Omoo*:

> His early history, like that of many other heroes, was enveloped in the profoundest obscurity; though he threw out hints of a patrimonial estate, a nabob uncle, and an unfortunate affair which sent him a-roving. All that was known, however, was this. He had gone out to Sydney as assistant-surgeon of an emigrant ship. On his arrival there, he went back into the country, and after a few months' wanderings, returned to Sydney penniless, and entered as doctor aboard of the *Julia*. . . . And from whatever high estate Doctor Long Ghost might have fallen, he had certainly at some time or other spent money, drunk Burgundy, and associated with gentlemen.

With Dr. Long Ghost as companion, Melville became a "beachcomber," first at Papeete, then on the other islands. One of the places of special interest to them at Papeete was the Royal Mission Chapel, a huge shell-like structure seven hundred feet long and over fifty feet wide; it was supported by breadfruit-tree pillars, open on all sides, and thatched with pandanus leaves. It had three pulpits, all of

BELOW: Tahiti: visiting whalers, natives, and thatched shelter.
OPPOSITE: A meeting of missionaries and natives of Tahiti.

which had been used simultaneously at the first service in 1819. The Queen of Papeete professed conversion to Christianity, but her allegiance was mainly economic. In fact, her riotous life scandalized the British and American Protestant missionaries. France had recently forced the acceptance of Catholic missionaries, but the Protestants undermined their influence. The natives thought the Catholic priests necromancers, and their celibacy was a great puzzle to the Tahitian girls. Melville found the priests more congenial than the Protestants, especially Father Murphy, an Irishman trained in a French seminary, who always served him good French brandy.

In *Omoo* Melville described a Sunday at the Protestant Church of Coconuts. The natives looked very awkward in European garments, the women in long "gay calico draperies" and the men in hot, ill-fitting coats and pantaloons. The Polynesians were extremely animated, talking, laughing, and rustling their starched clothing. It was so noisy that the "placid old missionary" could not be heard, and a dozen strapping fellows in white shirts and no pants created a great commotion by racing around demanding quiet.

Melville had provided himself with an interpreter, from whom he learned that the sermon was mainly concerned with warning the girls against the sailors from the whaling ships: "Where they come from, no good people talk to 'em—just like dogs," the interpreter rendered in pidgin English—the only English at his

Melville took a very dim view of the influence of the Christian missionaries on the South Sea islanders.

command. Against the French priests: "Wicked priests here, too; and wicked idols in woman's clothes." The sermon ended with a strong plea to the *kannakas* to "bring pig and fruit" to the *mickonaree*. "Mickonaree do great deal for kannaka; kannaka do little for mickonaree. So, good friends, weave plenty of coconut baskets, fill 'em, and bring 'em to-morrow."

"No race upon earth," Melville decided, is "less disposed by nature to the monitions of Christianity than the people of the South Seas." They "can hardly even be said to reflect," and act upon impulse. Consequently, the missionaries did not attempt to teach them dogmas, but exerted great efforts to suppress their worship of idols, to curb their sexual freedom, to prohibit their uninhibited dances, and to make them ashamed of their nakedness. One lovely lass told Melville that she was "Mickonaree *ena*," patting her mouth, but by vivid gestures gave him to

understand that she was no "Mickonaree" in her carnal parts. The missionaries used "Kannakippers," a Tahitian corruption of "constables," to spy out and report wickedness: "At the dead of night prowling around the houses, and in the daytime hunting amorous couples in the groves." Offenders were sentenced to work on the Broom Road, a broad highway running around the island—and it was well kept up.

Melville and Dr. Long Ghost worked for a short time on a plantation run by two Yankees, but mostly they roamed from village to village where they were received with generous primitive hospitality. At Tamai they witnessed an "old fashioned 'hevar,'" a Tahitian dance, held secretly at night. But after a week of delightful entertainment, they had to flee suddenly to avoid capture by the Kannakippers. When they arrived at Taloo, their next stop, they found that the queen had sought refuge there, and was trying to recruit foreigners to help her expel the French usurpers. The beachcombers began to count on "a surgeon's commission for the doctor, and a lieutenancy for myself," but nothing came of the expected commissions.

After visiting a number of other villages, Melville grew tired of being a beachcomber—an "omoo," a wanderer—and resolved to keep a look-out for a whaler in need of recruits. At Eimeo he got his chance on the *Charles & Henry,* from

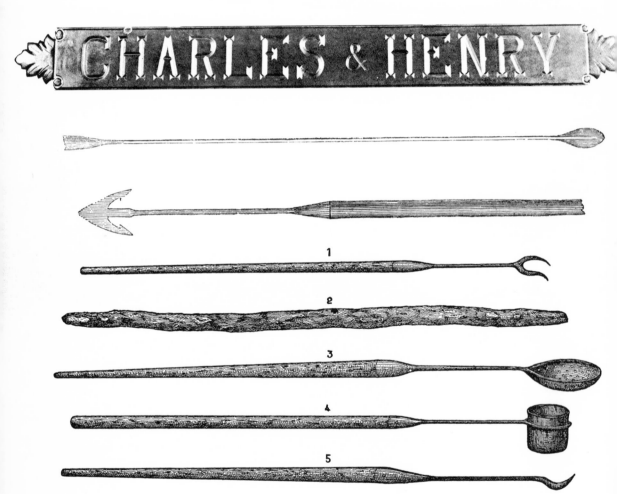

ABOVE: Harpooning whales in the Arctic Seas; probably the *Charles & Henry* did not go this far north. OPPOSITE ABOVE: Photograph of the centerboard of the whaler on which Melville left Tahiti. OPPOSITE BELOW: Whaling tools: harpoon and lance. Tools used in extracting oil from whale blubber: (1) blubber fork; (2) stirring pole; (3) skimmer; (4) bailer; (5) fire pike.

Nantucket. He liked the commander, John B. Coleman from Martha's Vineyard, "an uncommonly tall, robust, fine-looking man, in the prime of life," though perhaps fond of "sea-potations." On November 4, 1842, Melville signed the ship's articles, and collected an advance of fifteen Spanish dollars. He disliked parting with Dr. Long Ghost, but Captain Coleman suspected him of being a jailbird and would have nothing to do with him. Besides, the vagabond "doctor" was not yet tired of beachcombing.

Model whaleship and scrimshaw in Berkshire Athenaeum.

Captain Coleman had been very unlucky in capturing whales, and his cruise toward Japan was no more successful. He had taken only two hundred fifty barrels of sperm oil when he arrived at Lahaina, on Maui Island, the chief whaling port in Hawaii (then still called the Sandwich Islands) on April 27, 1843. This happened to be the day when the Maui Temperance Society was holding a meeting, attended by the king, the governor of the Island, and "a most respectable delegation of sea-faring men in port," as reported in the *Temperance Advocate and Seaman's Friend*. Melville made no comment on the temperance meeting. He went sight-seeing and saw the residence of the dowager queen, who had a reputation for savage ferocity. Melville claimed to have seen a hunchbacked retainer whose back she had broken over her knee twenty-five years earlier. But

ABOVE: Dr. Gerritt P. Judd, American missionary, who, as adviser to King Kamehameha III, largely controlled Honolulu during Melville's sojourn there. RIGHT: King Kamehameha III (1813–1854) sought protection and closer relations with the United States in 1843.

Lahaina in the Sandwich (Hawaiian) Islands was a favorite rendezvous for New Bedford whaling ships. Melville barely escaped being caught here by the captain of the *Acushnet*.

since then the royal family had come under the influence of the Christian missionaries. On coming to the throne in 1832, Kamehameha III had gone on a debauch that lasted several years, but the American missionaries now had him thoroughly under their control, and Dr. Gerritt P. Judd, as the king's adviser, was practically running the islands from Honolulu, on Oahu.

Melville was officially discharged from the *Charles & Henry* on May 4, in accordance with the agreement he had made in Tahiti, when the captain stopped for supplies in Honolulu. He had been wise—or lucky—to leave Lahaina without delay, for a week later the *Acushnet* arrived. He could still have been arrested for desertion if Captain Pease had caught him. In fact, on June 2 the captain filed a statement with the U.S. Vice Commercial Agent that Richard T. Greene and Herman Melville had deserted at Nuku Hiva on July 9, 1842, and five others later. One of the five had deserted at Lahaina the day after the *Acushnet* arrived. This ship also made a hasty visit to Honolulu on June 6, and Melville may have taken care to avoid meeting the crew. Fortunately she sailed again next day for the Japanese whaling grounds.

As in the Marquesas and Tahiti, it was Melville's luck to arrive in Honolulu during a political crisis. The previous February a dispute between English business-men and the Hawaiian king's advisers (American missionaries) had resulted in the seizure of the Sandwich Islands by Lord George Paulett in the name of Queen Victoria. King Kamehameha signed a provisional cession to prevent a threatened bombardment of Honolulu by British warships, but secretly sent a plea to President Tyler to intercede for him with Great Britain. The colonial expansion of

France in Polynesia had alarmed his advisers and they advocated annexation by the United States, but at that time the U.S. Senate was cold to the idea.

Under British authority the "blue laws" of the New England missionaries were relaxed. An editorial in the *Temperance Advocate and Seaman's Friend* dated July 24 complained:

> . . . Boat loads of lewd women have been seen going and returning from vessels which have recently touched at this Harbor for supplies. The law is prostrate . . . The most disgusting scenes are to be seen at noon-day in the streets of Honolulu, and around certain places of resort. Report of this state of things has drawn hither scores and hundreds of simple-minded and unwary females from the other Islands. . . .

Four days later Rear-Admiral Richard Thomas, Lord Paulett's superior, arrived in a frigate with authority from the British cabinet to restore the Sandwich Islands to King Kamehameha. On July 31 the British flag was hauled down, forty-two-pound cannon saluted the victory from Punchbowl Hill, and Honolulu began a celebration that lasted nearly two weeks. "It was a sort of Polynesian Saturnalia," Melville later stated in an Appendix to *Typee*. "Deeds too atrocious to be mentioned were done at noon-day in the open street. . . ."

Eventually order was restored, and the missionaries began to regain control. Though Melville had been shocked by the "Saturnalia," he did not become more sympathetic to the missionaries. In *Typee* he declared that "the natives have been civilized into draught horses, and evangelized into beasts of burden." He saw a hefty missionary wife being drawn in a cart by an old man and a youth. When they faltered on a steep hill she banged them over the head with her fan and yelled *"Hookee! Hookee!"* ("pull, pull"). Christianity, he concluded, had brought the Sandwich Islands only slavery. The Hawaiian population had vastly declined since the coming of the *haole*; they had lost their native arts and mores and were now a despondent, degraded people.

Melville spent about four months in Honolulu. He is reported to have been first employed as a pin boy in a bowling alley. On July 1 he was employed by a British merchant, Isaac Montgomery, as clerk and probably bookkeeper, contracting to work for a year at thirty-seven dollars and fifty cents a quarter, including board, lodging, and laundry. Apparently the arrangement was satisfactory to both parties, but Mr. Montgomery released his homesick clerk in August so that he might join the U.S. Navy and get transportation back to the United States.

The U.S. frigate *United States* arrived in Honolulu on August 3, 1843, on the day of a great *luau* at Nuana for the king. Americans hoped that the presence of

US Com'l Agency Lahaina:

I hereby certify that Valentine Pease 2d Master of the within named ship personally appeared before me & declared that — that David Smith deserted at Sakta, June 30th 1841, Richard T Green & Herman Mellvile deserted at Nukehiva July 9th 1842 — John Wright deserted at ditto Sept 14 " & Martin Brown at Rooapooa Sept 22 " & Jim Rosman deserted at Salango Feby 3d 1843 — I also certify that Henry Harmer deserted at this Port May 28th 1843 — In testimony of which I hereby subscribe my name & affix the Seal of this Agency this 2d day of June 1843

Jno Stetson
U.S.V Com'l agt

Certificate from Jno. Stetson, U.S.V. Consul Agt., given at Lahaina, Maui Island, Sandwich Islands, dated June 2, 1843, showing that *Herman Melville* and *Richard T. Green(e)* deserted the *Acushnet* at Nuku Hiva, Marquesas Islands, on July 9, 1842. Other men deserted at other places.

the great warship would help to dampen the riotous conduct of the natives, but probably the *United States* crew was one of the "two frigates" which Melville says was "let loose like so many demons." The Saturnalia had subsided by August 17, when Melville's name was added to the frigate's muster roll as an ordinary seaman, for three years of service or the length of the cruise.

On August 18, 1843, Melville witnessed flogging with the "kitten" on the deck of the U.S. Frigate *United States*.

Nearly everything on this warship was different from the whalers Melville had known, and he felt "half-stunned with the unaccustomed sounds ringing in his ears," the bells, the boatswain's whistle, the loud rumblings below deck. He was even more shaken next morning when the commander summoned the crew to witness the flogging of several men for drunkenness and other misdemeanors which shore leave had encouraged. The scene was still vivid in his memory nearly half a century later when he was writing *Billy Budd*—the bloody backs of the scourged men and the misery and shame in their faces. Though he would witness this horrifying spectacle frequently during the next fourteen months, he would never become hardened to it. He took extreme care not to incur such punishment himself.

On August 19 the *United States* sailed for Valparaiso and Callao by way of the Marquesas and Tahiti, under Commodore Thomas ap Catesby Jones. Melville was assigned the duty of ramming and sponging one of the big guns, very hot work in a tropical climate. But more appalling than swabbing a smoking cannon, or even seeing and hearing the lash of the "cat," was the monthly muster round the capstan to hear the captain's clerk read the "Articles of War." Of twenty offenses that a seaman could commit, thirteen were punishable by death. ". . . shall suffer death!" seemed the refrain to nearly every article—"no reservations, no contingencies . . . or reprieve . . . *shall suffer death! . . .*" Though Melville did not yet know it, on the U. S. *Somers* the previous November, his cousin Lieutenant Guert Gansevoort had taken part in trying and hanging the son of the secretary

Melville spent more than three years on ships and islands in the Pacific Ocean, rounding Cape Horn going west in April 1841 and going east in July 1844.

82

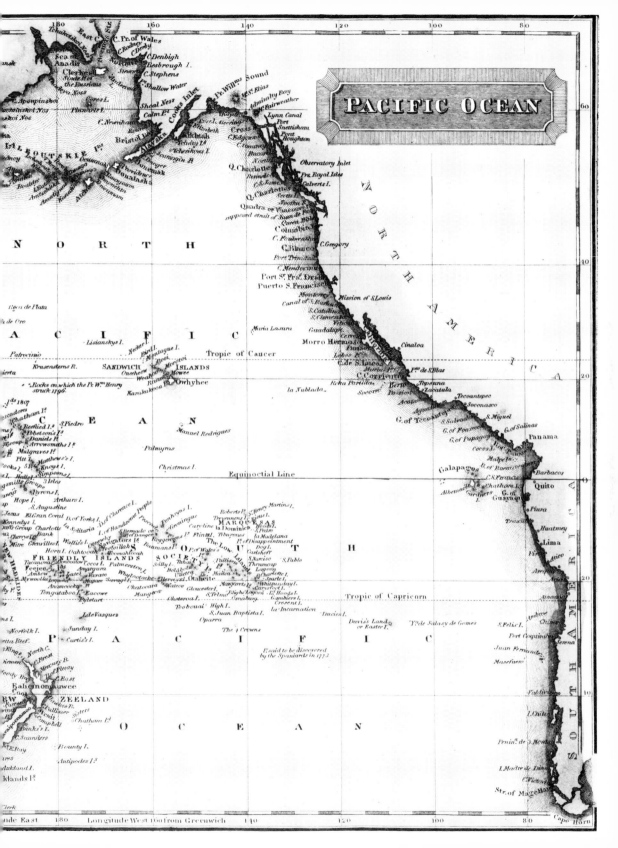

of war, who was accused of plotting mutiny. The political turmoil created by the execution had not yet died down.

Life aboard the *United States,* in spite of the naval discipline and arbitrary justice, was not all grimness and pain. Melville found several genial companions among the crew, best of all Jack Chase, Captain of the Top, a Briton, "true blue," with "a clear open-eye, a fine broad brow, and an abounding nut-brown beard." He could recite long passages from Byron, Scott, Shakespeare, and the epic sea poem the *Lusiad* in the original Portuguese. With Chase and other boon companions he enjoyed the amusing sights and experiences of the various ports.

On October 6 Melville saw *La Reine Blanche* again, anchored at Nuku Hiva. French sailors escorted the King and Queen of Nuku Hiva aboard the American frigate while the band played "King of the Cannibal Isles." Six weeks later the *United States* reached Valparaiso after an easy voyage from Tahiti, where Melville had not had time to look for Dr. Long Ghost. The ship then remained at Callao for seventy weary days. The only exciting thing that happened was a forty-eight-hour liberty, beginning on New Year's Day 1844, during which Melville and his starboard watch went to Lima, eight miles inland. Some hint of the impression Lima made on him can be found in the tragic imagery and allusions to this haunting city in his writings. He had heard much of the corruption of Lima, its deceitful women, crooked lotteries, swarming thieves, and lip-serving Catholics (perhaps the deeds of the latter were exaggerated by Protestant reports). He had heard, too, of the destructive earthquakes, the white buildings, and the arid climate. What he saw, he wrote later in *Moby Dick* (XLII), was "the rigid pallor of an apoplexy that fixed its own distortions."

The visit to Lima was the last of any significance in Melville's return home on the *United States.* In February 1844 his ship was sent to Mazatlán, Mexico, to obtain money to pay the squadron, but this was a rough, exhausting trip, and the crew was glad to get back to Callao on June 6. In their absence the commander of the Pacific Fleet had died, and this caused a general shifting of officers, with a new captain for the *United States,* but the return to Boston was only slightly delayed.

On June 20 Melville's starboard watch was given twenty-four hours of liberty in honor of Queen Victoria's accession to the throne of Great Britain. And the Fourth of July was celebrated by firing a salute from the big guns of the several warships in port. Two days later the *United States* sailed out of Callao. Rounding the Horn was rough, as expected, and for hours at a time the ship would bury herself at every plunge; then the wind would die down and the sails go slack, once for six hours, before another squall hit. Nevertheless, the rugged frigate made comparatively good time in her forty-one-day passage to Rio de Janeiro, arriving on August 16 and staying until August 24. In *White Jacket* Melville describes a shore leave at Rio, but the log of the ship shows no liberties in this harbor.

The *United States* arrived in Boston harbor on October 3, 1844, and anchored off the Navy Yard. After ten days of "breaking out and clearing out the ship," the crew was paid off, and Melville, having signed only for the cruise or for three years, was discharged, nearly four years after sailing from New Bedford. He immediately caught a steamboat for New York, where he found his brother Gansevoort just returned from an extensive political speaking tour through several states as he had been campaigning for James K. Polk.

James K. Polk.

Back at home with his family at Lansingburgh on the Hudson River, Herman's sisters and his youngest brother, Thomas, encouraged him to talk about his experiences, and with such a flatteringly attentive audience he reeled off his sailor yarns. Someone in the family suggested that he ought to write a book about his South Seas adventures with cannibals and Polynesian maidens. Why not indeed! It was a capital idea. But he had not kept diaries or notebooks, and when he began to write he found that he needed more information than he had in his memory; so he turned to the accounts of whaling captains and South Seas explorers to fill in where his information was scanty.

Both the research and the writing Melville found exhilarating, and later he declared to Hawthorne, "Until I was twenty-five, I had no development at all. From my twenty-fifth year I date my life." He did not, of course, mean his twenty-fifth birthday, which he had spent on a warship in the stormy seas off Cape Horn. His "life" began with the writing of his first book in the winter of 1844–1845. By spring he had a manuscript which he thought nearly finished. One of his sisters made a fair copy—his own handwriting was atrocious, and his spelling unreliable, even if he had been a schoolteacher—and he sent it to Harper & Brothers in New York. The first reader reported, "this work if not as good as *Robinson Crusoe* seems to be not far behind it." At an editorial conference, however, the firm decided not to publish it because "it was impossible that it could be true and therefore was without real value."

Gansevoort had also experienced frustration in securing a reward for his assistance in getting Polk elected President, but he was finally appointed Secretary of the U.S. Legation in London. Louis McLane, a former minister to Great Britain, was to be the new minister. When he left New York in the summer of 1845, Gansevoort took Herman's manuscript with him. A few months later he showed it to John Murray, one of the great British publishers of the period, who specialized in true travel accounts. Murray said it read like the work of "a practiced writer," not like a sailor who had never written before. Gansevoort assured him that his brother was a mere novice, and Murray finally paid one hundred pounds for the right to print an edition of one thousand copies.

In the absence of an international copyright law, it was then necessary to arrange simultaneous publication in Great Britain and the United States to prevent one country (more often the United States) from pirating the other's edition. In January 1846 George Putnam, partner in the American firm of Wiley & Putnam, was in London and he contracted for an American edition for one-half profits. Thus it came about that through his older brother's efforts Herman

Melville's book was published in London and New York in February 1846.

The British edition was called *Narrative of a Four Months' Residence Among the Natives of a Valley of the Marquesas Islands*; the American edition was called *Typee*, with a long subtitle. Melville dedicated the book to Lemuel Shaw, Chief Justice of the Commonwealth of Massachusetts, the lifelong friend of the Melville family and Herman's future father-in-law. Many reviewers in both countries questioned the truthfulness of the narrative, but most found it entertaining. Walt Whitman in the Brooklyn *Eagle* pronounced it "A strange, graceful, most readable book . . ." But in a few months American religious magazines began attacking *Typee* because of its unfavorable treatment of missionaries in Tahiti and the Sandwich Islands.

One of the readers of *Typee* was Richard Tobias Greene, the "Toby" who had deserted the *Acushnet* with Melville. To a reporter for a Buffalo newspaper he declared, "I am the true and veritable 'Toby,' yet living, and I am happy to testify to the entire accuracy of the work, so long as I was with Melville. . . ." Of course, the author was delighted to have this confirmation of his veracity. He visited Toby in Buffalo and prepared a "Sequel" to appear in the second edition of *Typee*. He also deleted his sharp comments on missionaries to satisfy Mr. Wiley, who had become extremely disturbed over the criticism of his firm in the religious press.

John Murray was not especially disturbed over the missionary question, though he accepted Melville's suggestion that a second British edition be based on the revised American one. He continued to have doubts about the truthfulness of the *Narratives*, and he asked for "documentary evidence" that Melville had lived in the Marquesas. Melville replied that he had requested a copy of the *Acushnet* log from the owners of the ship (and he did receive it several years later), but he said that obtaining any documents from the Typees was impossible; documents were unknown to them. Then he added: "Typees [*sic*] honesty must at last be beleived [*sic*] on its own account—they believe it here now—a little touched up they say but *true*."

One unexpected effect of *Typee* was to induce Herman's brother, Tom, to join a whaling cruise on March 14, 1846, at the age of sixteen. But Gansevoort, who had done so much to get the book published in both countries, did not live to enjoy its success. After a brief illness he died on May 12, 1846, in his London apartment, at the age of thirty. Herman wrote to President Polk to ask that the government bear the expenses of shipping the body home for burial, because, "Our family are in exceedingly embarrassed circumstances . . ." The request was granted, and on June 27 Herman transferred the coffin from the packet ship *Prince Albert* in New York harbor to the steamboat *Hendrik Hudson*, and accompanied it to Uncle Peter's house in Albany, where funeral services were held.

Melville continued the story of his South Seas wanderings in *Omoo*, which was published by Harper in late April and by Murray around May 1. Herman dedicated this book to his uncle "Herman Gansevoort, of Gansevoort, Saratoga County, New York . . ." To the reviewer in *Blackwood's Magazine* this dedication sounded like a spoof: "Of the existence of Uncle Gansevoort, of Gansevoort, Saratoga County, we are wholly incredulous." In general, reviewers worried less about whether the book was truth or fiction and, like Walt Whitman, recommended it for "entertainment." Of course the critics in the religious press were more unhappy than ever, for missionaries received even harder knocks in this book. But, more important to the author, he received assurances that it was selling. *Omoo* earned him over two thousand dollars in its first year, compared to nineteen hundred dollars for the first year of *Typee*.

The year he published *Omoo* Melville enjoyed his greatest literary success—perhaps, indeed, it was the happiest year of his life. But he had problems, nevertheless. He was engaged to marry Elizabeth Shaw, the adored friend of his sisters. He also knew that now he must be the chief support of his mother, for his brother Allan (born in 1823) was still trying to build a practice in law, while Tom might not be heard from for several years.

Melville applied for a clerkship with the United States Treasury Department, and went to Washington in February to press his application, but had no success. While in the capital he attended a session of the Twenty-ninth Congress, thereby obtaining impressions for future use. As a spectator in the gallery of the Senate, he was shocked and disillusioned to observe the senators paying no attention to the speaker. They laughed, chatted, picked their teeth, chewed tobacco and spat in the direction of large spittoons (a boorish habit which shocked Dickens on his visit to the United States), walked around, or dozed at their desks.

Early in 1847 Evert Duyckinck, with the support of Wiley & Putnam, started a weekly magazine called *The Literary World*. Though an editor for Wiley & Putnam, Duyckinck did not share Mr. Wiley's abhorrence of *Omoo* and published extracts in his magazine. He had also become a personal friend of the author, who for the next several years would be a frequent visitor at 20 Clinton Place, Duyckinck's residence in lower Manhattan. One of Evert's friends, Cornelius Mathews, became editor of the satirical magazine *Yankee Doodle* (modeled on the British *Punch*), and in July began publishing a series of humorous articles by Melville called "Authentic Anecdotes of 'Old Zack.'" General Zachary Taylor was becoming a national hero because of his victories in Mexico, and his eccentric manners had already made him a folksy legend. Taylor was a Whig and Melville was amused by the discomfiture of President Polk, who feared "Old Zack's" growing political appeal—with cause, as the next Presidential election proved.

General Zachary Taylor.

But for Melville the most important event in 1847 was his marriage in August to Elizabeth Shaw, the judge's third child by his first wife. She was three years younger than Herman, an attractive but by no means beautiful brunette, sensible, intelligent without being intellectual—in short, a *"nice* Boston girl," bearing little resemblance to the Polynesian Fayaway in *Typee*. Herman had known Elizabeth Shaw since childhood, but his courtship had begun after his return from his South Seas adventures. Before the wedding Judge Shaw gave Elizabeth and Herman three thousand dollars on which to start married life.

OPPOSITE: Elizabeth Shaw, whom Melville married in 1847. LEFT: Judge Lemuel Shaw, Chief Justice of Massachusetts, Melville's generous father-in-law.

Views of the ten locks on the Erie Canal in the village of Lockport.

The honeymoon trip was by train to New Hampshire and then by stage to Canada—Montreal and Quebec—with leisurely stops. The bride and groom returned by way of Lake Champlain and a night ride on an Erie Canal boat to Troy, an hour by train from Lansingburgh. They arrived at Mrs. Melville's home on August 27 before the family was awake, but, "We were very warmly welcomed and cared for and soon forgot the tribulations of our canal boat," Lizzy wrote her stepmother.

A month later Herman's brother Allan married and together they bought a house at 103 Fourth Avenue in New York City. There, according to plan, their mother and four sisters joined them at the end of September. In Lansingburgh Herman had begun a Polynesian sequel to *Typee-Omoo*, and he now settled down to work hard on it, in spite of social distractions. Evert Duyckinck wrote to his brother George: "Melville has got into a happier valley than the Happar not far from here [four blocks] and wife and I have looked in at the Ti [*house* in *Typee*]—

two very pretty parlors odorous of taste and domestic felicity. He is a right pleasant man to pass an evening with and I think I may promise you some pleasure from his society." Melville not only enjoyed the excellent wine and cuisine at 20 Clinton Place, but also, even more, the privilege of borrowing books from Evert Duyckinck's extensive library.

The reading of books would change Melville's professional career—in fact, wreck it. From Duyckinck he borrowed Sir Thomas Browne's *Religio Medici*, and pronounced the author a "cracked Archangel." He was also fascinated by Rabelais, Burton's *Anatomy of Melancholy*, and Spenser's *Faerie Queene*, and his fascination began to have a powerful effect on his imagination. He had started his new book, finally published as *Mardi*, as another sea romance in the South Seas, but after a few chapters it turned into an intricate allegory—philosophical and satirical, political and social.

In January 1848 Melville wrote to Murray that his new book would contain "in one cluster all that is romantic, whimsical, and poetic in Polynesia." Murray was wary because he had lost more money on *Omoo* than he had made on *Typee*. Two months later, in another attempt to sell his book to Murray, Melville said it was a downright "Romance of Polynesian Adventure." He had grown tired of factual narrative and had yielded to the longing "to plume my powers for [an imaginative] flight." This was exactly what he did in writing *Mardi*. It begins as if it were a continuation of the *Typee-Omoo* kind of adventures, with a new set of characters, and then enters a wholly make-believe world. The satirical chapters return to contemporary America in dispute with Great Britain over territory (the Oregon boundary), puffed up with pride in being "the best and happiest land under the sun," and the freest nation in all history. Yet in "The Great Central Temple" (the national Capitol) a black man wears an iron collar around his neck, and his back is streaked with red stripes like the striped "tappa" (flag) his master requires him to hoist as a symbol of the free nation.

This part of the satire might have appealed to the critics of slavery, but the author was not a social reformer because he believed that "though all evils may be assuaged, all evils can not be done away. For evil is the chronic malady of the universe; and checked in one place, breaks forth in another." Most readers of *Mardi* were simply bewildered by the journey from the real world into a symbolical one. Those who could understand the allegory were repelled by its pessimism and despair. *Mardi* very nearly lost Melville all the readers he had left after publishing *Omoo*. Bentley, not Murray, published it in London in March 1849 and Harper in New York in April.

Elizabeth Shaw Melville and her first child, Malcolm, in 1850.

Herman and Elizabeth's first child, a son (christened Malcolm), was born in February 1849. Even before *Mardi* was published Melville realized that he must quickly write something that would sell, and the reviews of *Mardi* intensified this conviction. He decided to write the most straightforward, unadorned narrative he could about his youthful round-trip cruise to Liverpool in 1839. This was *Redburn*, dedicated to "My Younger Brother/ Thomas Melville/ By Now a

Sailor on a Voyage to China." It was published in September 1849 in London and two months later in New York. Critics were relieved to find that the author had returned to his *Typee* style, and he regained some of his vanishing audience.

With scarcely a pause Melville launched into another unaffected narrative based on his life in the frigate *United States*. Abuses in the United States Navy were being debated in Congress, and there was a ready audience for an exposé of the cruelties which Melville had witnessed and abhorred during his brief navy career. As in *Typee*, he supplemented fact with imagination, but *White-Jacket* was basically true-to-life, vivid, and readable.

In spite of Bentley's disappointment with *Mardi*, he was interested in publishing *White-Jacket*—*Redburn* had restored his faith in the author. But Parliament had passed a law denying copyright to foreign authors whose countries did not reciprocate in protecting British authors, and the United States did not. Reputable British publishers tried not to take advantage of their American authors because of this law, especially Murray and Bentley, but the situation was confused and Bentley was slow in reaching a decision; consequently Melville decided that he should bargain in person. As he prepared to sail he wrote his father-in-law on October 6, 1849: "They [*White-Jacket* and *Redburn*] are two *jobs*, which I have done for money—being forced to it, as other men are to sawing wood."

Steamships were now making the run to England in two weeks, but Melville could save one hundred dollars each way by taking a packet, which would take a week longer. Besides, he liked a square-rigged, three-deck sailing ship, such as the *Southampton*, which he boarded on October 11. The captain of a packet associated with his passengers, and the accompanying farmyard (before refrigeration, live cows, pigs, and poultry were kept in pens on top of the main hatches of packet ships) made the *Southampton* seem almost like the *St. Lawrence* of ten years earlier. Melville quickly made friends with the captain and two passengers, Professor George Adler, a German philologist of New York University, and Dr. Franklin Taylor, a cousin of the famous travel writer Bayard Taylor.

Many nights, sustained by whisky punches, Melville talked German metaphysics with these two companions until two o'clock in the morning. He was now almost obsessed with the subject of "fixed fate and free will." Having been brought up in the Dutch Reformed Church, he had heard ministers expound predestination since his childhood. By the time he became a professional writer, he was consciously anti-Calvinist, but the idea of "fixed fate" had sunk in deeper than he realized. He was predisposed to "the power of blackness" before he read Hawthorne, but Hawthorne's tragic view of life confirmed his own experiences and intuitions, and Schopenhauer's pessimistic writings hardened his philosophical pessimism.

Every morning Melville exercised by climbing into the rigging, to the amusement of other passengers. One night, during a storm that made the ship roll and pitch so that Melville could not sleep, he dressed and went on deck. The captain showed him "corposant balls" on the yardarms and mastheads, a phenomenon he had never seen before—but would remember later in writing *Moby Dick*.

On November 4 Melville wrote in his diary: "'This time tomorrow I shall be on land, & press English earth after the lapse of ten years—*then* a sailor, *now* H.M. author of 'Peedee' 'Hullabaloo' & 'Pog-Dog.'" This sarcastic comment reveals how much "H.M." had changed since writing his first two books. Ten days later in London he wrote to Evert Duyckinck to thank him for a favorable review (which he said he had not read) of *Redburn*, "for it puts money into an empty purse," then added: "But I hope I shall never write such a book again—Tho' when a poor devil writes with duns all round him . . . what can you expect of that poor devil?—What but a beggarly 'Redburn'!"

Melville proposed to Professor Adler and Dr. Taylor that they disembark at Dover (actually Deal) and walk to Canterbury—eighteen miles—letting their baggage go on to London. However, after walking to Sandwich they stopped for breakfast, then took a train to Canterbury, and another train to London that afternoon. In London Melville became an indefatigable sight-seer, and through both Bentley and Murray received many social invitations. Bentley paid him two hundred pounds for a first edition of *White-Jacket*, thus enabling him to visit Paris, Brussels, Cologne, and Coblenz before returning to London in mid-December, where he was now almost lionized. He bought many books, visited art galleries, and would have had a splendid time if he had not been homesick for Lizzy and his infant son, Malcolm. Reluctantly he declined an invitation to visit the Duke of Rutland at his country estate and embarked for home on the packet *Independence* at Portsmouth on Christmas Day. To Bentley he wrote that he carried "the savor of the plum-puddings & roast turkey all the way across the Atlantic."

The *Independence* took more than a month to cross the Atlantic and it was not until February 1, 1850, that Melville reached home. The trip had been successful both personally and financially, and he was in a favorable frame of mind to begin the most important creative period of his life. Stimulated by the suggestion of his friend Richard Henry Dana, Jr., author of *Two Years Before the Mast*, that he do for the whaling industry what he had done for the navy, he began to borrow books about whales and whaling and to plan what at the time was simply a narrative of a "Whaling Voyage." But at an early stage he began to draw upon the legends of the fabulous whale "Mocha" or "Moby Dick," and before long he was calling his book "The Whale." The captain, too, was at first only an eccentric old whaler, but he also began to grow into mythical proportions. Thus, from a narrative like *White-Jacket*, the manuscript gradually took on the semblance of an epic, an allegory, and a tragic drama.

Aside from Melville's trying to write in a noisy house in the heart of the city, the spring of 1850 seemed propitious for his new book. *Redburn* and *White-Jacket* surprised him by their sales. But Malcolm was teething, Herman's sister-in-law was expecting her second child, which would increase the household to seven women and three babies, and Lizzy dreaded another hot summer in New York. In July Melville visited his Aunt Mary and cousin Robert in Pittsfield, perhaps intending to look into the possibility of moving there. After Uncle Thomas's death in Illinois, his widow had returned to the old farm in Pittsfield,

"Broadhall" in Pittsfield, Mass., where Melville visited his Uncle Thomas Melvill; Herman and his family vacationed here in August 1850.

ABOVE: Monument Mountain, near Stockbridge, Mass., where Melville and literary friends picnicked in August 1850. OPPOSITE: In 1850 Nathaniel Hawthorne and his wife, Sophia Peabody, then living at Stockbridge, became Melville's friends.

and recently she and her son had opened the shabby old mansion to summer boarders and called it Melville House—soon to be renamed "Broadhall" by its new owners.

Melville was so delighted with this rural retreat that he went back to New York to invite Evert Duyckinck and Cornelius Mathews to join him for a house party, and with his wife planned a masquerade ball to which they would invite some of the famous writers who had summer homes nearby in the Berkshires, including Dr. Oliver Wendell Holmes, William Cullen Bryant, the publisher James Fields and his bride, and a few others. Before the house party was over, Melville met Nathaniel Hawthorne, who was living only six miles away at Stockbridge. He had recently published *The Scarlet Letter* and was working on *The House of the Seven Gables*. He found Hawthorne the most stimulating man he had ever met, though there did seem to be something lacking in "the plump sphericity of the man."

Someone gave Melville a copy of *Mosses from an Old Manse*, which he read for the first time, and he was so enthusiastic about it that Duyckinck urged him to write an essay on it for the *Literary Messenger*. What Melville found so exciting in Hawthorne's book was "the power of blackness." In his essay he also defended nationality in literature, exaggerated almost to burlesque as a consequence of a discussion with his guests on a picnic. But it was Hawthorne's tragic sense of life that most impressed and influenced Melville.

Herman's Aunt Mary had promised to sell Broadhall to John Morewood before Melville's visit, but he discovered that he could buy the adjoining one-hundred-and-sixty-acre farm, with a rambling house and outbuildings, for sixty-five hundred dollars. With a loan of three thousand dollars from his father-in-law and a mortgage, he completed the deal and moved his family, including his mother and sisters, to the new home at the end of September. He named the place "Arrowhead" for the Indian arrow flints he found in the fields. Most of the land was in woods, and Melville intended to preserve the trees, though he would cultivate a few of the cleared acres to provide pasture and hay and corn for a cow and one or two horses. All the buildings were in a run-down condition and Melville began making needed repairs before settling down to writing. On a bright Sunday in October he wrote Evert Duyckinck: "I tell you that sunrises & sunsets grow side by side in these woods, & momentarily moult in the falling leaves.—A hammer? Yes a hammer is before me—and the very one that so cruelly bruised the very finger that guides my pen."

Farmer Melville established a consistent routine for himself. He rose at eight, went to the barn to feed his horse and "cut up a pumpkin or two" for his cow. Then he had his own breakfast, after which he lighted a fire in his "work-room" and wrote steadily until two-thirty, when his wife knocked on the door to signal that it was time for dinner. But before dining himself, he returned to the stable to give his horse and cow their dinner. "My own dinner over," he wrote Duyckinck, "I rig my sleigh & with my mother and sisters start off for the village . . . ," about two miles away. Not being able to write at night because of his weak eyes, he spent the evening in "a sort of mesmeric state" in his room. His mind was teeming with literary projects, and he wished he had about "fifty fast-writing youths" to take down his rapid flow of thoughts.

During the winter of 1850–1851 Melville reread Hawthorne's works, and there were occasional visits back and forth between the two families. In April, after reading *The House of the Seven Gables*, he wrote Hawthorne that he had never encountered another mind with so intense a feeling for "the visible truth . . . the apprehension of the absolute condition of present things as they strike the eye of

101

ABOVE: "These mountains, somehow, they play at hide-
and-seek, and all before one's eyes."—"The Piazza."
RIGHT: "Arrowhead" interior after it became a museum.

the man who fears them not, though they do their worst to him . . . " This statement could almost characterize Melville's Captain Ahab, the demented old man who was taking over the whaling story and turning it into a tragedy. At the end of May Melville assured Hawthorne that his "Whale" was "in his flurry," and that he would soon "take him by the jaw . . . and finish him up . . . " But this was said partly in disillusionment, for he added: "What's the use of elaborating what, in its very essence, is so short-lived as a modern book? Though I wrote the Gospels in this century, I should die in the gutter."

Melville was indeed writing something like a modern Gospel, for his whale had become, at least to his monomaniac Ahab, a symbol of ultimate truth, or the invisible source of all visible reality. Carlyle's "philosophy of clothes" in *Sartor Resartus* had influenced this symbolism, and Hawthorne's fiction had taught him how to use physical images to symbolize psychological and spiritual "truths." Some readers would see in the narrator, Ishmael, an "isolato" like his creator, Melville in disguise, and Melville did give him many of his own experiences and sentiments as a sailor. But something of an author's own character goes into all his fantasy people: Ishmael says that Ahab's "quenchless feud" with the white whale (which meant also with God–nature–destiny) is his, and vicariously it was the author's. But Ishmael is not so much a participant as a spectator to the tragic encounter, and so was Melville to the "visible truth." Yet so intimate and personal to the author was the feud between Ahab and Moby Dick that he could not finish it off by simple will power. At the end of June Melville wrote Hawthorne: "The tail is not yet cooked—though the hell-fire in which the whole book is broiled might not unreasonably have cooked it all ere this."

While Melville was trying to finish his tragedy in which the fabulous whale sank the *Pequod*, the ship that had served as his model was wrecked in the North Pacific, not by a whale but the elements. On her third voyage, the *Acushnet* was lost on August 16, 1851, off Saint Lawrence Island, though news did not reach the United States until several month later. Fourteen American whaling ships were wrecked that stormy summer.

Meanwhile, Melville took time out from his writing to plant a garden and some fields of potatoes, corn, pumpkins, and other edibles for his family and his domestic animals, and to plow and hoe at needed intervals, but the "cooking" of the allegorical whale continued throughout the summer. By August Bentley had promised one hundred fifty pounds and one-half profits, and in September Allan Melville, now acting as Herman's agent and attorney, negotiated terms with Harper & Brothers. After shipping the American proof sheets to Bentley, Melville

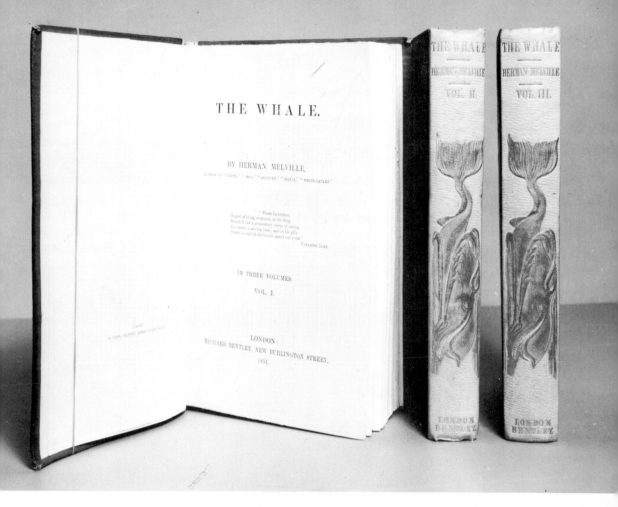

London edition of *Moby Dick*, in three volumes, bore Melville's first title, *The Whale*.

decided to call the book *Moby Dick*, and Allan wrote Bentley to change the title of the English edition, but it was published as *The Whale*.

Melville dedicated the book to Hawthorne, who wrote a letter of appreciation (unfortunately lost, with his other letters to Melville) that Melville called "my glorious gratuity"; he felt "an unspeakable security" because of Hawthorne's "having understood the book." Then he confessed: "I have written a wicked book, and feel spotless as the lamb." A French critic acutely observed that Ahab wanted to harpoon Moby Dick because he could not harpoon God, and perhaps this was what Melville himself meant in his statement to Hawthorne.

To Mrs. Hawthorne, Melville insisted that he had not consciously written *Moby Dick* as an allegory: "I had some vague idea while writing it, that the whole book was susceptible of an allegoric construction, & also that *parts* of it were—but the speciality of many of the particular subordinate allegories, were first revealed to me, after reading Mr. Hawthorne's letter . . . " In other words, he had employed symbols as they occurred to him, but had not deliberately integrated them into an over-all schemata.

Most reviewers of *Moby Dick* were baffled, some incensed, and nearly all disappointed. A critic in the *Democratic Review* felt "imposed upon": the author "is gauging, at once, our gullibility and our patience . . . " Herman Melville had written one of the greatest masterpieces of fiction in the history of American literature, yet he had good reason to fear that he "might die in the gutter." About the same time he was giving birth to this book, his wife gave birth to her second child, a son, who was named Stanwix.

In January 1852, before Melville knew that *Moby Dick* would be an economic failure, he had assured Mrs. Hawthorne that his next book would be a "rural bowl of milk." But this phrase hardly characterizes *Pierre*, though it was possible that the reviews of *Moby Dick* would curdle the milk. At any rate, something curdled it, for *Pierre* was not only bitter about society and skeptical of the nature of man, it also insinuated sexual themes which were absolutely taboo in mid-nineteenth-century American literature.

Pierre bore the subtitle *or, The Ambiguities*, and indeed nearly everything in the novel is ambiguous. The first ambiguity is the Arcadian setting of the rural estate of the widowed Mrs. Glendinning, where she lives with her nineteen-year-old son. To each other they use the language of lovers instead of mother and son. Pierre is engaged to Lucy Tartan, a blond beauty chosen by Mrs. Glendinning to be her son's bride. But he discovers that a mysterious dark-haired girl, Isabel, born in a foreign country (like Herman's cousin Marie) is probably his illegitimate half sister, begotten by his father during his travels. To protect her he "elopes" with her to New York, though intending to keep the relationship platonic. Pierre thinks he is acting from the most unselfish motives, but finds Isabel so sexually tempting that he begins to doubt the "purity" of his motives. That they are guilty of incest is delicately insinuated.

On the way to the city Pierre finds a tract, by a religious fanatic named Plinlimmon, who symbolizes the morality of the world and ideal or Christ-like morality as two kinds of "time." The world lives by Greenwich or relative time; the completely unselfish person lives by heavenly time. The point of the conceit is the impossibility for a finite mortal to live by celestial morality. And Pierre finds this to be true. The book contains a great deal of unambiguous satire on hypocrisy, contemporary taste in literature, and social evils of the period, but the hypocrisy of a "pure heart" seems to be the central motif. Pierre is betrayed by his mother, his cousin, and his own impulses to do good. His mother dies of wounded pride, Pierre murders his cousin, and he, Isabel, and Lucy commit suicide. Contemporary literary critics found the melodramatic plot, the moral pessimism, and the implications of incest intolerable—and few people bought the book.

The state of excitement in which Melville wrote *Pierre* and his disappointment in its reception after its publication in 1852 resulted in nervous exhaustion, which became so acute in the spring of 1853 that his wife had him examined by Dr. Holmes, who assured her that he was tired but not insane. However, she became convinced that he must have a respite from literary labor and began beseeching

Herman Melville's children: Stanwix, Frances ("Fanny"), Malcolm, and Elizabeth ("Bessie").

friends and relatives to find other employment for him. Hawthorne had written a campaign biography for Franklin Pierce and been rewarded with a consulship in Liverpool. He tried to use his influence to get President Pierce to appoint Melville to a similar post, but Melville had done nothing to curry political favor. Meanwhile, his responsibilities increased and his means of meeting them diminished. In 1853 Mrs. Melville gave birth to her third child, a daughter, whom they named Elizabeth. In December a fire in the Harper warehouse destroyed their stock of Melville's books, and there was not enough demand to justify reprinting them. Fortunately, he was able for the next three years to earn some money by contributing stories and sketches to the newly founded *Putnam's Monthly Magazine* and *Harper's New Monthly Magazine.*

All of Melville's publications now reflected his increasing sense of neglect and failure. In 1855 he published a reworking of the biography of Israel Potter, which he had bought in England in 1849. The story was that of a New England farm boy who fought heroically at Bunker Hill, was captured and taken to England, became a courier for Benjamin Franklin between Paris and England, and served in the United States Navy under the fabulous John Paul Jones—only to become marooned in England for fifty years. In his old age Potter finally got back home to find his family gone, a great hole in the ground where the house once stood, and himself presumed dead. As a veteran of the American Revolution, he applied to Congress for a pension, but it was rejected for lack of documentary evidence, and he remained a forgotten man. Although Melville used the anonymous biography for the basic story, he added a great many passages to turn a rather flat narrative into a witty and sardonic tale.

In 1856 Melville finished his last novel, *The Confidence-Man,* though it was not published until the following year. The setting is a steamboat on the Mississippi River, with descriptions of places Melville had evidently seen on his trip west in 1840. The Confidence Man wears many disguises, but always swindles someone into giving money for a nonexistent orphanage, investing in a fraudulent coal mine, or having "confidence" in some other fake enterprise, such as Dickens had satirized in *Martin Chuzzlewit.* In this book Melville's satire is so all-embracing that everything appears to be a "confidence game": society, politics, business, religion, the Bible, perhaps human life itself. In the final chapter a senile old man, who suspiciously resembles the popular image of God, has to be led to his stateroom by the Confidence Man in his last disguise as a "Cosmopolitan": ". . . the waning light expired, and with it the waning flames of the horned altar, and the waning halo round the robed man's brow; while in the darkness which ensued, the Cosmopolitan kindly led the old man away . . . " This dark and pessimistic allegory was so unacceptable to an habitually optimistic nation that it seems, in retrospect, almost contrived to end Herman Melville's literary career, and to all practical purposes it did.

Melville's sympathetic father-in-law shared his daughter's concern for Herman's health, and in the autumn of 1856 sent him fifteen hundred dollars to enable him to make a trip to the Mediterranean. In mid-October he sailed for England in the propeller-driven steamship *Glasgow*. After landing at Glasgow, he visited Edinburgh and its environs (remembering his Scotch ancestry), and then called on Hawthorne at the consulate in Liverpool. The Hawthornes were about to leave for a seaside vacation at Southport, in Lancashire, and they invited Melville to join them, which he did. To Hawthorne he seemed depressed and careworn. In his *Journal* Hawthorne wrote:

> . . . we took a pretty long walk together, and sat down in a hollow among the sand hills (sheltering ourselves from the high, cool wind) and smoked a cigar. Melville, as he always does, began to reason of Providence and futurity, and of everything that lies beyond human ken, and informed me that he had "pretty much made up his mind to be annihilated"; but still he does not seem to rest in that anticipation; and, I think, will never rest until he gets hold of a definite belief. . . . He can neither believe, nor be comfortable in his disbelief . . . If he were a religious man, he would be one of the most truly religious and reverential . . .

On November 18 Melville sailed for London, taking only a carpetbag and leaving his trunk with Hawthorne, who commented in his *Journal*: "He learned his travelling habits by drifting about, all over the South Seas, with no other clothes or equipage than a red flannel shirt and a pair of duck trowsers. Yet we seldom see men of less criticizable manners than he."

Melville kept a journal of his trip, and scrupulously recorded his impressions of every city and country he visited: Syria, Salonica, Jerusalem, Joppa, Beirut, Athens, Naples, Rome (in this order), and his return by train through Italy, Switzerland, northern Germany, Holland, and boarding a steamer at Rotterdam for London. Alexandria bored him, but Cairo was like a "Bartholomew Fair—a grand masquerade of mortality." The ruined mosques and crumbling houses were depressing. He had never seen so many blind men in his life, with flies crawling on their eyes at noon: "Nature feeding on men." The pyramids, too, were both appalling and fascinating: "A feeling of awe & terror" came over him as an Arab conducted him into a dusty side hole "like a coal-shaft":

. . . The stooping & doubling. I shudder at idea of ancient Egyptians. It was in these pyramids that was conceived the idea of Jehovah. Terrible mixture of the cunning and awful. Moses learned in all the lore of the Egyptians. The idea of Jehovah born here.—When I was at top, thought it not so high—sat down on edge. Looked below—gradual nervousness & final giddiness & terror. . . . After seeing the pyramids, all other architecture seems but pastry.

Palestine made similar contradictory impressions on Melville. At Bethany he visited a wretched Arab village. Brook Kedron looked "black and funereal." From

BELOW: Church of the Holy Sepulcher in Jerusalem: "A sort of plague-stricken splendor reigns in the painted & mildewed walls around."—Melville's *Journal Up the Straits*. OPPOSITE: Through Via Dolorosa Melville retraced Christ's steps from Pilate's judgment hall to Golgotha.

Jericho he rode over a "mouldy plain" to the Dead Sea which reminded him of the "bitterness of life" and death. The landscape of Judea was bleached a leprosy white, an "encrustation of curses . . . refuse & rubbish of creation. . . . We read a good deal about stones in Scriptures. . . . And no wonder . . . Judea is one accumulation of stones . . . " Stony mountains and plains, "stony eyes and stony hearts."

Of all places visited, Jerusalem affected Melville most. This city seemed "expressive of the finality of Christianity, as if this was the last religion of the world— no other, possible." He rose every morning at dawn and went exploring. At the Holy Sepulcher Turkish policemen sat "crosslegged & smoking, scornfully observing the continuous troups of pilgrims entering & prostrating themselves before the anointing-stone of Christ, which veined with streaks of a mouldy red looks like a butcher's slab." Melville concluded that "the diabolical landscape of Judea must have suggested to the Jewish prophets, their ghastly theology." And he wondered, "Is the desolation of the land the result of the fatal embrace of the Deity? Hapless are the favorites of heaven."

While Melville was in Rome his brother Allan negotiated a contract with Longman and Green to publish *The Confidence-Man* in London (Herman had signed a contract with Dix & Edwards for an American edition before leaving New York), and the book was being reviewed in England when he arrived in London on April 26, but he made no comment about reviews in his journal; perhaps he didn't read them. After sight-seeing and visiting art galleries, he went to Oxford: "It was here I first confessed with gratitude my mother land, & hailed her with pride." Then he went by stage to Warwick, greatly admiring the beauty of the countryside, and by train to Birmingham and to Liverpool—"Like riding through burnt

111

LEFT: At Bethany, Melville visited a "wretched Arab village . . . ."—*Journal*. BELOW: Mosque of Omar in Jerusalem, guarded by Turkish soldiers at the time of Melville's visit. OPPOSITE: The road to the Mount of Olives, overlooking Jerusalem.

district." Having retrieved his trunk from Hawthorne, he boarded the *City of Manchester* on May 5 and arrived in New York two weeks later.

For three years after his return from the Mediterranean trip Melville tried to earn a living by giving lectures; it was the heyday of the public lecturer in America, and some authors earned more on the platform than at their writing desks. But Melville insisted on talking about "The Statuary of Rome" instead of his experiences in the South Seas, in which there was a popular interest. He said he would not repeat his books, and that he had really lost interest in the subject matter of his early books. Discouraged by lecturing, he eagerly accepted an invitation from his brother Tom, now the captain-owner of the clipper ship *Meteor*, to accompany him to San Francisco—and perhaps to Asia. At the end of May he boarded the ship in Boston, with great anticipations of pleasure, but the first day out he was seasick—a discouraging beginning. At the end of June the ship crossed the "Line." On Melville's birthday (August 1), they encountered their first severe gale, with worse ones to follow as they approached the Strait of Le Maire. During the short day in that latitude they could see land on both sides: "Horrible snowy mountains —black, thunder-cloud woods—gorges—hell-landscapes." During a gale with mixed snow and sleet, a young man from Nantucket fell from a yardarm while trying to furl a topsail and was killed. After a terrific struggle they finally got around the Horn and sailed without further difficulty to San Francisco, where the *Meteor* anchored October 11. By Pony Express Herman wrote Lizzy that he had not been benefited by the trip as much as he expected and would return by steamer to Panama, take a train across the Isthmus, and then board another steamer for New York.

Early in 1861 Melville made an attempt to secure the consulship in Florence, going again to Washington to further his candidacy. He attended a levee in the White House and shook hands with the President: "Old Abe is much better looking [than] I expected & younger looking," he wrote his wife. "He shook hands like a good fellow—working hard at it like a man sawing wood at so much per cord." But the consulship in Florence went to William Dean Howells as a reward for writing the campaign life of Lincoln.

The execution of John Brown in 1859 seemed to Herman Melville an ominous "portent" of greater tragic events to follow, and he wrote this poem entitled "The Portent":

> Hanging from the beam,
>   Slowly swaying (such the law),
> Gaunt the shadow on your green,

In 1860 Herman Melville sailed with his brother Thomas to San Francisco

Shenandoah!
The cut is on the crown
    (Lo, John Brown),
And the stabs shall heal no more.

Hidden in the cap
    Is the anguish none can draw;
So your future veils its face,
    Shenandoah!
But the streaming beard is shown
    (Weird John Brown),
The Meteor of the war.

Melville had been secretly writing poetry for several years, and before sailing on the *Meteor* had left a book in manuscript with his brother Allan, who was not able to find a publisher. Nevertheless, Melville continued to write poems during the Civil War, and these show the torment of doubt and increasing pessimism which the war caused him to feel. In a note to "The Conflict of Convictions" he explained the mood in which he wrote the poem:

> The gloomy lull of the early part of the winter of 1860–61, seeming big with final disaster to our institutions, affected some minds that believed them to constitute one of the great hopes of mankind, much as the eclipse which came over the promise of the first French Revolution affected kindred natures, throwing them for the time into doubts and misgivings universal.

In the poem Melville hoped that "a wind in purpose strong" might be spinning *"against* the way it drives." But he had little faith that good would come out of the impending tragedy. Even if the North were successful, as he expected it to be, he feared that it would be corrupted by the victory, a truly prophetic insight as the "Gilded Age" would demonstrate.

    Power unanointed may come—
Dominion (unsought by the free)
    And the Iron Dome [of the national Capitol],
Stronger for stress and strain,
Fling her huge shadow athwart the main;
But the Founders' dream shall flee.

Melville was not one of those who saw a Divine Purpose being carried out in the Civil War. Rather, he saw God as keeping "the middle way," favoring neither

116   OPPOSITE AND OVERLEAF: Aboard Capt. Thomas Melville's clipper ship the *Meteor*, Melville wrote
fatherly letter to his elder daughter instructing her to hold "Fanny's" hand when they went up the hi
(Elizabeth was seven, Frances five.)

Pacific Ocean
Sep. 2ᵈ 1860

My Dear Bessie: I thought
I would send you a letter, that
you could read yourself — at
least a part of it. But here and
there I purpose to write in the usual
manner, as I find the printing style
comes rather awkwardly in a rolling ship.
Mamma will read these parts to you. We
have seen a good many
sea-birds. Many have follo-
-wed the ship day after day.
I used to feed them with
crumbs. But now it has got
to be warm weather, the birds
have left us. They were about
as big as chickens — They were
all over speckled — and they would

sometimes, during a calm, keep behind
the ship, fluttering along on the water,
with a mighty cackling, and whenever
anything was thrown overboard they would
hurry to get it. But they never would
light on the ship — They kept all the
time flying or else resting themselves
by floating on the water like ducks
in a pond. These birds have no
home, unless it is some wild rocks
in the middle of the ocean. They never
see any orchards, and have a taste of
the apples & cherries, like your gay little
friend in Pittsfield — Robin Red Breast Esq
— I could tell you a good
many more things about the sea, but I
I must defer the rest till I get home.

I hope you are a
good girl; and give Mama
no trouble. Do you help
Mama keep house?

That little bag you made for me, I use very often, and think of you every time.

I suppose you have had a good many walks on the hill, and picked the strawberries.

I hope you take good care of little

FANNY

and that when you go on the hill, you go this way:

That is to say, hand in hand.

By-by

Papa.

one side nor the other for, "NONE WAS BY/WHEN HE SPREAD THE SKY:/WISDOM IS VAIN, AND PROPHECY."

When in 1861 the Union Navy tried to seal off the Charleston harbor by sinking old whale ships filled with stones, Melville wrote "The Stone Fleet: An Old Sailor's Lament." He had "a feeling for those ships" because he had "scudded round the Horn in one . . ." And it was "all for naught. The waters pass—/ Currents will have their way;/ Nature is nobody's ally . . ." In a prose afterword appended to *Battle-Pieces* (1866) Melville urged the victorious North to show mercy and compassion to the vanquished South instead of a spirit of continued revenge. This plea was praised by some critics, but the versification of the poems was too rough and "prosy" to win wide approval. Today *Battle-Pieces* is rated second only to Whitman's *Drum-Taps* in Civil War poetry, but this was not true during Melville's lifetime.

In December 1866 Melville finally obtained an appointment as an inspector of customs in the New York harbor. By curious coincidence, he was for some years stationed at the foot of Gansevoort Street on the North River (Hudson). One day he dropped into Gansevoort Hotel and asked the man at the tobacco counter about the name of the hotel. An old gentleman, hearing the question, spoke up: "Sir, this hotel and the street of the same name are called after a very rich family who in old times owned a great deal of property hereabouts." The reply caused Melville to moralize "upon the instability of human glory . . ."

But the unwealthy grandson of the Gansevoorts was thankful for his humble position. His duty was to make a personal examination of the cargo of ships arriving in his district, work which kept him much in the open air—in all kinds of weather, winter and summer. Later he was shifted to the East River in the Bronx borough. Except for holidays, illness, and a two-week vacation each summer, Melville made his daily rounds for nineteen years—until the will of Mrs. Ellen Marett Gifford enabled him to retire on December 31, 1885. Mrs. Gifford was the daughter of a business associate who had been partly responsible for the bankruptcy of Melville's father in 1830, and apparently her father's conduct was on her conscience. She left Mrs. Melville ten thousand dollars (plus an additional five thousand dollars in a codicil), Herman eight thousand dollars, and three thousand dollars to each of the Melville children.

During the nearly two decades of his career as a customs inspector, Melville's domestic life was embittered by disappointments with his two sons. Malcolm joined the National Guard and became obsessed with guns. He slept with a pistol

Herman Melville in 1861.

under his pillow, and in 1867, when he was eighteen, after a severe parental reprimand for keeping late hours, he was found in bed with a bullet hole in his temple. Whether suicide or accident his parents never really knew.

Stanwix, two years younger than Malcolm, was restless and was never able to settle down after finishing high school. Perhaps he wanted to emulate his father in his South Seas adventures, or his Uncle Thomas, the clipper ship captain. When he was twenty his parents consented to his shipping to China with a captain his Uncle Thomas knew. After his return he studied dentistry for a short period, but began wandering again—to Kansas, to New Orleans, to Cuba, to Central and South America, where he, too, became a beachcomber. Home again, he resumed dentistry (manufacture of plates), then went to California to work on a sheep ranch, contracted tuberculosis of the lungs, and died in a San Francisco hospital February 23, 1886. Melville's older daughter, Elizabeth ("Bessie"), suffered from chronic arthritis and never married. His younger daughter, Frances, married Henry B. Thomas and lived across the river in East Orange, New Jersey, in easy visiting distance.

In 1867 Thomas Melville retired from the sea and became governor of the Sailors Snug Harbor at New Brighton on Staten Island, a well-endowed asylum for sick and retired seamen. It consisted of a group of substantial white brick buildings on landscaped grounds overlooking the bay, and Herman's mother found Tom's new home more attractive than Herman's on 26th Street. In fact, Tom could now provide a home for her and his unmarried sisters to relieve Herman of the burden he had carried for so many years. At Thanksgiving and Christmas the two brothers and their families enjoyed festive dinners in the Sailors Snug Harbor. Mrs. Maria Gansevoort Melville lived at New Brighton until her death on April 1, 1872, at the age of eighty-one.

Melville had continued to write poetry while making his daily inspection of ships. In 1876 his Uncle Peter paid for a private edition of *Clarel*, a long poem of seven thousand lines based on Melville's trip to Palestine. Through the mouths of characters representing every religion, the poet debated the theological and philosophical subjects which had obsessed his mind ever since Hawthorne had known him. No one character, however, ever exhibits a faith that the author himself could accept. Writing *Clarel* caused Melville great anguish of mind and conscience and nearly exhausted him, as his wife revealed in letters to her relatives —always with sympathy and patience for her distraught husband. He wrote the poem in octosyllabic couplets, an inappropriate verse form for a long narrative poem. Melville himself said it was "eminently adapted for unpopularity," and this was a correct assessment.

Malcolm Melville in his National Guard uniform

In 1888 Melville published a private edition of poems called *John Marr and Other Sailors*. The central character, after many years as a sailor, has had to retire from maritime life because of a wound received in fighting pirates. He settles on the western prairie with a young wife, but a fever ends her life and that of her infant. Old Marr lives on alone, sustained by his memories, which he sometimes mentions to his neighbors, but they have never seen the ocean and cannot understand what he is talking about. The poet felt a sympathetic identification with the lonely old salt stranded high and dry hundreds of miles from the sound of the surf.

Melville's last years were not without some pleasures. In February 1888 he took his last sea voyage, a trip to Bermuda, with a stopover at Saint Augustine, Florida, on his return in March. And in July he took a vacation on Fire Island, which had become his wife's favorite vacation spot, partly because she suffered from rose fever—and Herman was a rose gardner. When he did not accompany her he became restless at home, though he had some enjoyments there, too. One was corresponding with several British admirers of his books, men who kept a spark of his reputation alive in England after it had almost become extinguished in his own country. One of these men was H. S. Salt, author of a biography of James Thomson, one of Melville's favorite poets (he called *City of Dreadful Night* the "modern book of Job"). Nearly all these British correspondents also admired Walt Whitman. In a letter to James Billson, Melville thanked him both for his article on Thomson and for sending Robert Buchanan's "tribute to Whitman." In a footnote to this tribute, a poem called "Socrates in Camden," Buchanan complained that he had sought Melville when on a visit to New York but no one in the city "seemed to know anything of the one great imaginative writer fit to stand shoulder to shoulder with Whitman on that continent." Melville had known of Whitman, of course, since his review of *Typee* and *Omoo* in the Brooklyn *Eagle*, and it is strange that these two half-Dutch authors from Brooklyn and New York never met. On February 1, 1888, E. C. Stedman, editor, critic, and minor poet, sent Melville the manuscript of his essay on Whitman for his forthcoming *Poets of America*, with the comment: "as you said so much of Whitman, I will run the risk of showing you my chapter on him . . ."

At the time of Melville's resignation from the Customs House post, his wife wrote Catherine Lansing, daughter of Herman's Uncle Peter: "He has a great deal unfinished work at his desk which will give him occupation, which together with his love of books prevent time from hanging heavy on his hands—and I hope he will get into a more quiet frame of mind . . ." His most important "unfinished

Maria Gansevoort Melville at the age of eighty.

ABOVE: The Gansevoort–Lansing Mansion in Albany. LEFT: Elizabeth Shaw Melville in 1885. BELOW: Herman Melville in 1885.

Melville's brothers: ABOVE LEFT: Allan, New York lawyer. ABOVE RIGHT: Thomas, Governor of Sailor's Snug Harbor on Staten Island after he retired as captain of a clipper ship.

Melville's sisters: LEFT: Catherine, married John C. Hoadley. RIGHT: Augusta, unmarried. BELOW LEFT: Frances Priscilla, unmarried. BELOW RIGHT: Helen, married George Griggs.

work" was a story about a handsome young sailor, Billy Budd, as unaware of evil as Adam before the "fall." He was falsely accused of treason by a villainous master-at-arms. Billy's one defect was a stammer when extremely excited; consequently, unable to reply verbally to the libel, he struck his accuser on the temple, killing him instantly. This took place in the presence of the captain, who exclaimed: "Struck dead by an angel of God! Yet the angel must hang!" Though the conspiracy charge might be false, striking an officer—let alone murdering him—was punishable by death according to the "Articles of War," which Captain Vere had sworn to uphold. Accordingly, he hastily summoned a drumhead court-martial and asked his first lieutenant to preside over it, though he, himself, did not remain neutral, for he exerted enormous pressure to get a conviction. They pronounced Billy guilty and he was sentenced to hang the next morning.

Very nearly this same drama had actually taken place in 1842 on the U.S. frigate *Somers*, under the command of Captain Mackenzie. And Melville's cousin Guert Gansevoort, as noted earlier, had been the first lieutenant who presided over the

BELOW: Melville lot in Albany Rural Cemetery, Menands, N.Y., showing tombstones of his father and mother, sister Catherine, and her husband. OPPOSITE: Walt Whitman, whom Melville never met but greatly admired.

drumhead court. The culprit was Philip Spencer, who happened to be the son of the secretary of war. Naturally there were repercussions—Congressional investigations, a warrant sworn out for Lieutenant Gansevoort's arrest while he was on leave in Albany, and great political agitation. This took place while Herman Melville was on his whaling trip, but of course he heard about it many times from his family, and no doubt from Guert himself. The suggestion has been made that Melville wrote the story to exonerate his cousin, but why would he wait fifty years? Besides, it does not exonerate anyone who sat on the drumhead court. Furthermore, Melville combined details from this American event with the setting of the great rebellion in the British Navy at the Nore in 1797. This not only provided "esthetic distance" but also enabled him to focus on the moral import of the story.

The night before Billy is hanged, he sleeps like a baby, and even the priest thinks it would be useless to persuade him to repent of a crime he could not understand. Before going to his death, he calls out a blessing on his captain. As he swings at the yardarm, the sun bursts through the fleecy clouds in "a soft glory as of the fleece of the Lamb of God seen in mystical vision." Many critics have interpreted this detail as a "transfiguration"—as one biographer puts it, "such as the apostle saw when he exclaimed, 'O death, where is thy sting?'" But Melville did not end the story here—and in fact the state of his manuscript leaves some doubt that he had finished it. He added an epilogue in which Billy becomes a legend in the navy, not as a victim of arbitrary naval justice (or injustice) but as a common criminal. This, Melville seems to be saying, is the justice not only of a man-of-war, but of a man-of-war world, to which he was no more reconciled than he had been to the "Articles of War" when he first heard them read on the frigate *United States.*

Mrs. Melville found the *Billy Budd* manuscripts (more than one version) in her husband's desk after his death, but it was not published until 1924, after a vigorous revival of interest in Melville was under way.

Herman Melville died on September 28, 1891, of "cardiac dilation." Most of the New York newspapers ignored his passing, but the *Press* printed a short article, which began:

> There died yesterday at his quiet home in this city a man who, although he had done almost no literary work during the past sixteen years, was once one of the most popular writers in the United States.
> Herman Melville probably reached the height of his fame about 1852, his first novel having been printed about 1847 [1846]. . . .

The New York *Daily Tribune* notice was only one paragraph, in which the

Melville's writing desk, now in Berkshire Athenaeum.

opinion was offered that *Typee* was Melville's best work. This judgment was not challenged until the "Melville revival" began about 1920. Today, there is no doubt that Robert Buchanan was right; he not only deserved in his lifetime to stand with Walt Whitman, but in the twentieth century he is regarded almost universally as the equal of Whitman or any other American author of the nineteenth century.

Bibliography

Works by Melville

Typee: A Peep at Polynesian Life. New York: Wiley & Putnam; London: John Murray, 1846.

Omoo: A Narrative of Adventures in the South Seas. New York: Harper & Brothers; London: John Murray, 1847.

Mardi and a Voyage Hither. London: Richard Bentley; New York: Harper & Brothers, 1849.

Redburn: His First Voyage. London: Richard Bentley; New York; Harper & Brothers, 1849.

White-Jacket; or The World in a Man-of-War. London: Richard Bentley, 1850; New York: Harper & Brothers, 1950.

The Whale. London: Richard Bentley; *Moby-Dick; or, The Whale.* New York: Harper & Brothers, 1851.

Pierre; or, The Ambiguities. New York: Harper & Brothers; London: Sampson, Low and Son, 1852.

Israel Potter: His Fifty Years of Exile. New York: G. P. Putnam and Sons, 1855.

The Piazza Tales. New York: Dix & Edwards, 1856.

The Confidence-Man: His Masquerade. New York: Dix & Edwards; London: Longman, Brown, Green, Longman, and Roberts, 1857.

Battle-Pieces and Aspects of the War. New York: Harper & Brothers, 1866. Edited with Introduction and Notes by Hennig Cohen, New York: Thomas Yoseloff, 1963.

Clarel: A Poem and a Pilgrimage in the Holy Land. New York: G. P. Putnam Sons, 1876.

John Marr and Other Sailors. New York: privately printed, 1888.

Timoleon. New York: privately printed, 1891.

Billy Budd, Foretopman. London: Constable and Co., 1924. Edited by Harrison Hayford and Merton M. Sealts, Jr., Chicago: University of Chicago Press, 1962.

The Works of Herman Melville. London: Constable and Co., 1922–1924. 16 vols.

A definitive edition of *The Writings of Herman Melville,* under the editorship of Harrison Hayford, Hershel Parker, and G. Thomas Tanselle is in process of publication by the Northwestern University Press and the Newberry Library in Chicago. Published to date: *Typee,* 1968; *Omoo,* 1968; and *Redburn,* 1969.

Journals, Letters, and Miscellaneous

Howard Vincent, ed. *Collected Poems of Herman Melville.* Chicago: Packard and Co., 1938.

Eleanor L. Metcalf, ed. *Journals of a Visit to London and the Continent by Herman Melville*. Cambridge: Harvard University Press, 1948.

Jay Leyda, ed. *The Melville Log: A Documentary Life of Herman Melville*. New York: Harcourt, Brace and Co., 1951. 2 vols.

Eleanor Melville Metcalf. *Herman Melville: Cycle and Epicycle*. Cambridge: Harvard University Press, 1953.

Howard C. Horsford, ed. *Journal of a Visit to Europe and the Levant*. Princeton: Princeton University Press, 1955.

Merrell R. Davis and William H. Gilman, eds. *The Letters of Herman Melville*. New Haven: Yale University Press, 1960.

Biographies

Raymond M. Weaver. *Herman Melville: Mariner and Mystic*. New York: George H. Doran Co., 1921.

Lewis Mumford. *Herman Melville*. New York: Harcourt, Brace and Co., 1929.

Newton Arvin. *Herman Melville*. New York: William Sloane Associates, 1950.

Leon Howard. *Herman Melville*. Berkeley: University of California Press, 1951.

William H. Gilman. *Melville's Early Life and Redburn*. New York: New York University Press, 1951.

Critical Studies

Charles Anderson. *Melville in the South Seas*. New York: Columbia University Press, 1939; New York: Dover Publications, Inc., 1966.

Charles Olsen. *Call Me Ishmael*. New York: Reynal & Hitchcock, 1947.

Richard Chace. *Herman Melville: A Critical Study*. New York: Macmillan and Co., 1949.

Howard R. Vincent. *The Trying-Out of Moby-Dick*. Boston: Houghton Mifflin Co., 1949.

Lawrance Thompson. *Melville's Quarrel with God*. Princeton, Princeton University Press, 1952.

James Baird. *Ishmael*. Baltimore: Johns Hopkins Press, 1956.

Milton R. Stern. *The Fine Hammered Steel of Herman Melville*. Urbana: University of Illinois Press, 1957.

James E. Miller, Jr. *A Reader's Guide to Herman Melville*. New York: Farrar, Straus and Cudahy (Noonday ser.), 1962.

Hershel Parker. *The Recognition of Herman Melville*. Ann Arbor: University of Michigan Press, 1967.

Chronology

1819   Herman Melville was born August 1, 1819, at 6 Pearl Street in New York City, the third child and second son of Allan Melvill (later spelled *Melville*) and Maria Gansevoort M. The father was an importer of French dry goods.

1820   Mrs. Allan Melvill and her children spent the summer with her Gansevoort relatives in Albany, New York. In September she brought them back to a new home at 55 Courtlandt Street.

1824   In March the Melvill family moved to 33 Bleecker Street. Herman began attending school but was not fond of books.

1826   Herman had scarlet fever (probably the cause of his weak eyes later). Allan Melvill's business suffered from the stagnant national economy.

1827   Herman became a monitor in New York Male High School, to the surprise of his father, who thought his older son, Gansevoort, the student of the family. Allan Melvill borrowed money from his father and brother-in-law, Peter Gansevoort, trying to save his business.

1828   Herman was declared the best speaker in his school. The family moved to Broadway, between Bond and Great Jones Streets.

1829   During school vacation in August Herman visited his grandfather, Major Thomas Melvill, in Boston.

1830   Allan Melvill failed in his New York business and moved to Albany. His family was entirely dependent upon Peter Gansevoort for support. Herman attended Albany Academy. His grandmother, Catherine Van Schaick Gansevoort, died, but Mrs. Allan Melvill's inheritance was tied up by legal action for several years.

1831   Herman won first prize in his class for bookkeeping. On a business trip to New York Allan Melvill suffered from exposure and became ill.

1832   Allan Melvill became delirious, and died on January 28. Herman and Gansevoort withdrew from Albany Academy; Gansevoort opened a fur and cap store; Herman clerked in his Uncle Peter's bank.

1833   Gansevoort added an *e* to the family name, and other members of his family adopted the new spelling. Herman vacationed in August on his Uncle Thomas's farm at Pittsfield, Massachusetts.

1834   For seven or eight months, beginning in the summer, Herman worked on his Uncle Thomas Melvill's Pittsfield farm.

1835   In spring (?) Herman began attending Albany Classical School and clerking after school hours in his brother's store.

1837   A financial panic in April forced Gansevoort Melville to close his business. Herman tried to revive the Philologos [Debating] Society in Albany and as a consequence got into a bitter newspaper quarrel with its former president, continuing into 1838. In autumn Herman taught a country school near Pittsfield, Massachusetts.

1838   On November 12 Herman enrolled in Lansingburgh Academy to study surveying. His mother had recently moved to Lansingburgh.

1839   In April Herman failed to secure employment on the Erie Canal as a surveyor. In May he contributed "Fragments from a Writing Desk" to the *Democratic Press and Lansingburgh Advertiser*. On June 5 he sailed for Liverpool on the *St. Lawrence* as a "boy," arrived there July 4, and returned to New York September 30. In October he began teaching in another country school at Greenbush, New York.

1840   On June 4 he started west, probably expecting to find employment in Illinois, where his Uncle Thomas had recently settled, but returned to New York in September. On December 31 in New Bedford, Massachusetts, he signed on the whaling ship *Acushnet* for a voyage to the South Seas.

1841   January 3 the *Acushnet* sailed from Fairhaven, reached Rio de Janeiro March 13 and the Horn April 15. In the autumn the *Acushnet* cruised in the region of the Galápagos Islands and crossed the equator on October 24.

1842   On June 23 the *Acushnet* anchored in Nuku Hiva Bay in the Marquesas. On July 9 Melville and Richard Tobias ("Toby") Greene deserted and set out for the Happar natives but reached the valley of the Typees, reported to be cannibals. Melville was crippled by a leg injury and Toby left him to get help. After about three weeks with the Typees, Melville was rescued by the crew of the whaler *Lucy Ann*, which reached Tahiti in mid-September. Melville took part in another rebellion and was imprisoned in Tahiti for several weeks. After being freed, he roamed the islands with "Dr. Long Ghost" until November 4, when he signed on the *Charles & Henry* for a cruise to the Japanese whaling grounds.

1843   The *Charles & Henry* arrived at Lahaina, Sandwich Islands [Hawaiian Islands] on April 27, reached Honolulu May 4, where Melville was discharged and on June 1 became a bookkeeper for a merchant. On August 17 he joined the United States Navy and left Honolulu in the crew of the U.S. frigate *United States*. On October 6 he saw Nuku Hiva again, and Tahiti on October 12. The warship reached Valparaiso November 21 and Callao December 15.

1844   After delays the *United States* finally sailed for Boston July 6 and arrived October 3. Melville was discharged from the Navy October 14. He returned to Lansingburgh in November.

1845   During the spring Melville began writing about his adventures in the South Pacific. July 30 Gansevoort Melville, newly appointed secretary of the United States Legation in London, sailed with part of the manuscript of *Typee*. John Murray had to be assured the work was not fiction before he accepted it for publication.

1846   *Typee* was published in London by Murray in February and in New York the same month by Wiley & Putnam. The book was favorably reviewed in both countries, though some critics doubted its authenticity. Tobias Greene turned up to corroborate the truth of the narrative. Wiley and Putnam insisted on deletions in a second edition.

1847   *Omoo*, a sequel to *Typee*, was published in April by Harper & Brothers and in

May by John Murray. The religious press was exercised over Melville's criticism of Christian missions in Tahiti and Hawaii. On August 4 Melville married Elizabeth Shaw in Boston. In September they established a home in New York at 103 Fourth Avenue with Herman's brother Allan and his bride.

1848   Melville began *Mardi* as another South Seas adventure but turned it into a highly symbolical allegory.

1849   Herman and Elizabeth Melville's first son, whom they named Malcolm, was born February 16. Melville began reading and annotating a large-type edition of Shakespeare. *Mardi* was published in March by Richard Bentley in London and in April by Harper & Brothers in New York. Most reviewers were hostile and Melville's reputation began to decline. In September Bentley published *Redburn*, based on Melville's voyage to Liverpool in 1839; Harper published the American edition. On October 11 Melville sailed for London to arrange publication of *White-Jacket,* based on his Navy experiences. He started for New York on Christmas Day.

1850   Melville vacationed in Pittsfield in the summer and on August 6 he and his wife picknicked on Monument Mountain with Hawthorne, Dr. Oliver Wendell Holmes, Evert Duyckinck, and others. The Melville family became intimate with the Hawthorne family. Herman bought a farm at Pittsfield and moved his family, including his mother and sisters, there early in October. He had begun *The Whale* (later *Moby Dick*) in New York and by December 16 in Pittsfield had reached chapter 85.

1851   In May Melville had to stop writing to plant his farm, but managed to finish *The Whale* in July. His second child, Stanwix, was born October 22. Bentley published *The Whale* in October and Harper *Moby Dick* (a last-minute change of title) in November. Reviews were mixed and sales disappointing.

1852   *Pierre; or, The Ambiguities,* was published by Harper in August, and in London by Sampson, Low & Son in November, Bentley having declined this melodramatic novel. It received bad reviews and nearly ruined Melville's remaining literary reputation.

1853   On May 22 the Melvilles' third child and first daughter was born—named Elizabeth (Bessie). Melville's friends made another attempt to secure a consulship for him. *Putnam's Monthly Magazine* published "Bartleby the Scrivener" in November and December. A fire in Harper's warehouse on December 10 destroyed all copies of Melville's books, thus stopping all income from Harper's.

1854   *Putnam's* published "The Encantadas" in March, April, and May. *Harper's New Monthly Magazine* also began publishing stories and sketches by Melville.

1855   G. P. Putnam Sons published *Israel Potter* in April. Melville's daughter Frances, fourth and last child, born March 2.

1856   Dix & Edwards published *Piazza Tales* in April. Melville sailed from New York to Glasgow on October 11. He visited Hawthorne in Liverpool in November and from London continued his trip to the Mediterranean and Palestine.

1857   Dix & Edwards published *The Confidence-Man* in April. Melville sailed from Liverpool May 5 and arrived in New York May 20.

1857–1860 Melville attempted to lecture, with indifferent success, on "Statuary in Rome" and classical mythology.

1860 Melville sailed May 30 for San Francisco on the clipper *Meteor,* owned and captained by his brother Thomas. The trip did not improve his health and he returned in the autumn by way of the Isthmus of Panama and a steamship from New Granada.

1861 Melville's friends made another futile attempt to secure a consulship for him.

1863 In the spring Melville sold his Pittsfield farm, Arrowhead, to his brother Allan and bought a house at 104 East 26th Street in New York.

1866 Harper published *Battle-Pieces* in the summer. December 6 Melville became District Inspector of Customs in New York, stationed at 207 West Street, on the Hudson River.

1867 Melville's son Malcolm shot himself on September 11, whether intentionally was never known. Herman's brother Thomas became Governor of the Sailors Snug Harbor on Staten Island and Maria Gansevoort Melville and his sisters began living with him. For several years family reunions were held on Staten Island.

1872 Melville's brother Allan died February 9 "in great agony." Melville's son Stanwix began wandering. April 1 Maria Gansevoort Melville died on Staten Island. August 4 Herman and Elizabeth Melville observed their twenty-fifth wedding anniversary in Pittsfield.

1874 Melville's niece Maria married William B. Morewood on June 10.

1876 Melville's sister Augusta died on April 4. *Clarel* was published in June by G.P. Putnam Sons—got mixed reviews.

1884 March 5 Melville's brother Thomas died.

1885 Melville's sister Frances Priscilla died on July 9. On December 31, having received a small inheritance, Melville resigned as customs inspector.

1886 Melville's son Stanwix died in San Francisco February 23.

1888 September 7 *John Marr and Other Sailors* was privately printed (twenty-five copies). November 16 Melville began writing *Billy Budd.*

1891 Melville completed *Billy Budd* in April; in June he had *Timoleon* privately printed (twenty-five copies). September 28 he suffered a fatal heart attack in his home at 104 East 26th Street.

Stamp on Melville envelope.

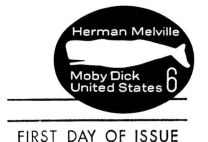

Herman Melville
Moby Dick
United States 6

FIRST DAY OF ISSUE

Title page "The Harpooner Prepares to Strike"; painting by Sir Oswald Brierly, c. 1868. Kendall Whaling Museum, Lynn, Mass. *Photo Eric H. Muller.*

4 Sunday afternoon on the Battery; three-panel lithograph by Thomas Thompson, 1829. Courtesy Picture Collection, New York Public Library.

7 Herman Melville; portrait in oil by Joseph Oriel Eaton, 1870, in the Houghton Library of Harvard University. By permission of the Houghton Library and Fogg Museum.

8 Whaleship. Courtesy Picture Collection, New York Public Library.

11 The East River from the New York side, c. 1835; lithograph in the Stokes Collection, New York Public Library.

12 Herman Melville's mother, Maria Gansevoort, before her marriage; painting from the Gansevoort-Lansing Collection, New York Public Library.

Herman Melville's father, Allan Melvill; watercolor portrait by John Rubens Smith (American artist), Paris, 1810. Metropolitan Museum of Art, New York, bequest of Miss Charlotte E. Hoadley, 1946.

13 Priscilla (Mrs. Thomas) Melvill, Melville's paternal grandmother; portrait by Francis Alexander. Courtesy The Bostonian Society, Old State House.

Home of Major Thomas Melvill; painting dated 1832. Courtesy The Bostonian Society, Old State House.

14 Melville's maternal grandfather, General Peter Gansevoort. Courtesy Gansevoort-Lansing Collection, New York Public Library.

Catherine Gansevoort, Melville's maternal grandmother. Courtesy Gansevoort-Lansing Collection, New York Public Library.

15 Allan Melvill; oil portrait by Ezra Ames, c. 1820. By permission of the Henry E. Huntington Library and Art Gallery, San Marino, Calif.

16 Maria (Mrs. Allan) Melville; oil portrait by Ezra Ames, c. 1820. By permission of the Berkshire Athenaeum, Pittsfield, Mass.

17 Steamboat *Albany*; woodcut from the Albany Institute of History and Art.

18 New York Harbor from Bedloe's Island in the early 1880s. Courtesy Picture Collection, New York Public Library.

20 Susan (Mrs. Peter) Gansevoort. Courtesy Gansevoort-Lansing Collection, New York Public Library.

Peter Gansevoort. Courtesy Gansevoort-Lansing Collection, New York Public Library.

21 *"Ville d'Albany, Capitale de l'état de New-York"*; drawing by J. Milbert. Lithograph from the Albany Institute of History and Art.

22 Fashionable upper Broadway; etching by T. Horner. Courtesy Stokes Collection, New York Public Library.

23 Melville house on Market Street, Albany. Courtesy Albany Institute of History and Art.

24 The fashion center of Albany. Courtesy Albany Institute of History and Art.

25 A grocery store in Albany. Courtesy Albany Institute of History and Art.

27 Clinton Park and North Pearl Street. Courtesy Albany Institute of History and Art.

28 Albany Academy. Courtesy Albany Institute of History and Art.

Albany Female Academy. Courtesy Albany Institute of History and Art.

29 State Bank of Albany, owned by Peter Gansevoort. Courtesy Albany Institute of History and Art.

31 The great fire in New York City, 1835; lithograph from the Stokes Collection, New York Public Library.

32 Gansevoort Melville. Courtesy Gansevoort-Lansing Collection, New York Public Library.

Lansingburgh residence of the Melville family; watercolor by Frances D. (Mrs. Warren J.) Broderick, 1969. *Photo Warren F. Broderick.*

Lansingburgh Academy; pen and ink sketch by Frances D. Broderick, 1969. *Photo Warren F. Broderick.*

33 Lansingburgh on the Hudson; woodcut in the collection of Frances D. Broderick.

34 Lower Broadway; lithograph from the Stokes Collection, New York Public Library.

35 South Street in 1850; scale model by Samuel H. Gottscho. Museum of the City of New York.

37 "American Ships in the Mersey"; painting by R. Salmon. Courtesy Walker Art Gallery, Liverpool.

38 "New Bedford"; unsigned American watercolor, 1835. Courtesy Kendall Whaling Museum, Lynn, Mass. *Photo Eric H. Muller.*

39 New York Harbor as seen from the Bay in 1835; painting by J. G. Chapman. Courtesy Stokes Collection, New York Public Library.

40 The Battery; panoramic painting by Samuel B. Waugh, 1847. Museum of the City of New York.

41 Cenotaph in the Seamen's Bethel at New Bedford. Courtesy of The Whaling Museum, New Bedford, Mass.

45 Steamboats on the Mississippi.

46 Architect's drawing for the *Acushnet*. Melville Collection, Houghton Library, Harvard University. *Photo Fogg Museum.*

47 Crew list of the *Acushnet*. Houghton Library, Harvard University.

51 "A Pod of Sperm Whales"; oil painting by J. R. Winn, 1862. Kendall Whaling Museum, Lynn, Mass. *Photo Eric H. Muller.*

52 "Whaling in the South Seas"; American watercolor by W. Copeland, c. 1865. Kendall Whaling Museum, Lynn, Mass. *Photo Eric H. Muller.*

53 A wounded whale chewing up a whaleboat; woodcut dated 1850 from the Picture Collection, New York Public Library.

55 "The Power of a Sperm Whale's Flukes"; American oil by C. S. Raleigh, 1877. Kendall Whaling Museum, Lynn, Mass.

56 Rock Rodondo; painting by Toft. By permission of the Berkshire Athenaeum.

58 Capturing Galápagos tortoises; woodcut from *Harper's New Monthly Magazine*, August 1859.

60 Typee Bay. Courtesy of The Whaling Museum, New Bedford, Mass.

62 Marquesan "whinhenies" and sailors; picture from *Voyage autour du monde sur la frégate "La Venus"* . . . *Atlas pittoresque* by Abel Du Petit-Thouars, 1841. *Photo Bernice P. Bishop Museum, Honolulu.*

63 Richard T. Greene. By permission of the Berkshire Athenaeum.

65 "Resolution Bay in the Marquesas"; drawn by W. Hodges. Picture from *Voyage autour du monde sur la frégate "La Venus"* . . . *Atlas pittoresque* by Abel Du Petit-Thouars, 1841. *Photo Bernice P. Bishop Museum, Honolulu.*

66 A scene on or near Tahiti, perhaps the district of Matavai. From the collection of Frances D. Broderick. *Photo Warren F. Broderick.*

67 View on Tahiti, c. 1840. From the collection of Frances D. Broderick. *Photo Warren F. Broderick.*

68 Tahiti: visiting whalers, natives, and thatched shelter. From the collection of Frances D. Broderick. *Photo Warren F. Broderick.*

69 Missionaries and Tahitians; woodcut, probably from *Polynesean Researches* by William Ellis, in the collection of Frances D. Broderick. *Photo Warren F. Broderick.*

71 "Noukahiva, 1823"; watercolor by **Max Radiguet**. *Photo Bernice P. Bishop Museum, Honolulu.*

72 Centerboard of the *Charles & Henry*. Courtesy Old Dartmouth Historical Society, New Bedford, Mass.

Whaling tools: harpoon and lance. Courtesy Picture Collection, New York Public Library.

Tools used in extracting oil from whale blubber. Courtesy Picture Collection, New York Public Library.

73 "Harpooning the Whale in the Arctic Seas, for Lamp Oil"; drawing, courtesy Picture Collection, New York Public Library.

75 Model whaleship and scrimshaw; display in the Berkshire Athenaeum.

76 Dr. Gerritt P. Judd. *Photo Bernice P. Bishop Museum, Honolulu.*

King Kamehameha III. *Photo Bernice P. Bishop Museum, Honolulu.*

77 "New Bedford Whaleships at Lahaina in the Hawaiian Islands"; painting in The Whaling Museum, New Bedford, Mass.

79 Certificate showing Melville's desertion from the *Acushnet*. Original in The Whaling Museum, New Bedford, Mass.

81 A flogging; probably a watercolor by William Meyers in *Abstract of a Cruise in* [ship] *United States*, 1843–44. Print in the collection of Frances D. Broderick. *Photo Warren F. Broderick.*

83 Pacific Ocean; from a map in *A New Universal Atlas of the World*, by J. and S. Morse, New Haven, 1822.

85 President James K. Polk. Brady Collection, National Archives.

89 General Zachary Taylor. Reproduced from the collections of the Library of Congress.

90 Judge Lemuel Shaw. Courtesy Gansevoort-Lansing Collection, New York Public Library.

91 Elizabeth Shaw. Courtesy Gansevoort-Lansing Collection, New York Public Library.

92 "View of the Upper Village of Lockport, Niagara Co., N.Y."; drawing by W. Wilson. Division of Maps, Library of Congress.

94 Elizabeth Shaw Melville and her first child, Malcolm, in 1850. Courtesy Gansevoort-Lansing Collection, New York Public Library.

97 "Broadhall." Courtesy Gansevoort-Lansing Collection, New York Public Library.

98 Monument Mountain, near Stockbridge, Mass. *Photograph by Edwin H. Miller, 1969.*

99 Nathaniel Hawthorne. Brady Colleclection, National Archives.

100 "Arrowhead"; drawing by Herman Melville. Original unlocated—reproduced from *Herman Melville: Mariner and Mystic,* by Raymond M. Weaver. New York: George H. Doran Co., 1921.

101 Sophia Peabody (Mrs. Nathaniel Hawthorne) in 1830. By permission of the Berkshire Athenaeum.

102 Berkshire scene: Greylock and Saddleback from "Arrowhead." By permission of the Berkshire Athenaeum.

103 Interior of "Arrowhead" after it became a museum; photograph taken 1897. By permission of the Berkshire Athenaeum.

105 London edition of *Moby Dick,* bearing Melville's first title, *The Whale.* Courtesy of the Houghton Library, Harvard University.

107 Herman Melville's children. Courtesy Gansevoort-Lansing Collection, New York Public Library.

110 Church of the Holy Sepulcher, Jerusalem. *Brown Brothers.*

111 Via Dolorosa. *Brown Brothers.*

112 Arab peasants. *Brown Brothers.*

Mosque of Omar, Jerusalem. *Brown Brothers.*

113 The road to the Mount of Olives, overlooking Jerusalem. *Brown Brothers.*

115 Melville and his brother Thomas; ambrotype by Davis, Boston. By permission of the Berkshire Athenaeum.

117– A letter Melville wrote to his daugh-
119 ter Elizabeth, September 2, 1860; holograph by permission of the Houghton Library, Harvard University.

121 Herman Melville in 1861; photograph by Rodney Dewey, Pittsfield. Courtesy of the Berkshire Athenaeum.

127 Maria Gansevort Melville at the age of eighty. Courtesy Gansevoort-Lansing Collection, New York Public Library.

126 The Gansevoort-Lansing Mansion in Albany. Courtesy Gansevoort-Lansing Collection, New York Public Library.

Elizabeth Shaw Melville in 1885. Courtesy Gansevoort-Lansing Collection, New York Public Library.

Herman Melville in 1885. Courtesy Gansevoort-Lansing Collection, New York Public Library.

127 Melville's sister Frances Priscilla. Courtesy Gansevoort-Lansing Collection, New York Public Library.

Melville's brother Thomas. Courtesy Gansevoort-Lansing Collection, New York Public Library.

Melville's brother Allan. Courtesy Gansevoort-Lansing Collection, New York Public Library.

Melville's sister Helen (Mrs. George Griggs). Courtesy Gansevoort-Lansing Collection, New York Public Library.

Melville's sister Catherine (Mrs. John C. Hoadley). Courtesy Gansevoort-Lansing Collection, New York Public Library.

Melville's sister Augusta. Courtesy Gansevoort-Lansing Collection, New York Public Library.

128 Melville Lot in Albany Rural Cemetery, Menands, N. Y. Collection of Frances D. Broderick. *Photo Mason Robinson.*

129 Walt Whitman. Brady Collection, National Archives.

131 Melville's passport and manuscript boxes. By permission of the Berkshire Athenaeum.

137 Stamp on Melville envelope. First day of issue, March 7, 1970.

Index

143

144